Published by Robert Kennedy Publishing
400 Matheson Boulevard West
Mississauga, ON
L5R 3M1 Canada
Visit us at www.rkpubs.com or www.musclemag.com

Art Director: Jason Branidis
Managing Director: Wendy Morley
Copy Editors: Jacqui Hartly
             Melissa Desousa
Proofreader: James De Medeiros
Cover Photos: Rich Baker of Marco Cardona
             ©iStockphoto.com/MMIAD

Library and Archives Canada Cataloguing in Publication

Thorne, Gerard, 1963-

Supersized! : a step-by-step 12-month musclebuilding course to take

you from beginner to advanced / Gerard Thorne.

Includes index.

ISBN 978-1-55210-102-5

1. Bodybuilding--Training. 2. Weight training. I. Title.

GV546.5.T487 2011   613.7'13   C2011-903047-0

10 9 8 7 6 5 4 3 2 1

Distributed in Canada by NBN (National Book Network)
67 Mowat Avenue, Suite 241
Toronto, ON
M6K 3E3

Distributed in USA by NBN (National Book Network)
15200 NBN Way
Blue Ridge Summit, PA
17214
Printed in Canada

WARNING

The information in this book reflects the author's experiences and opinions and is not meant to replace medical advice.

Before beginning this or any other nutritional or exercise regimen, consult your doctor to be sure it is right for you. Ask for a physical stress test.

SUP
SIZI

SUPERSIZED!

A step-by-step 12-month muscle-building course to take you from beginner to advanced

Photo by George Butler
Model Arnold Schwarzenegger

TABLE OF CONTENTS

8

ACKNOWLEDGMENTS

As with all publications it would not have been possible to produce this work without the generous assistance of various individuals.

It seems like it was just a few years ago that Robert Kennedy gave me the opportunity to contribute to his organization by writing the first *MuscleMag International Encyclopedia of Bodybuilding*. Who could have envisioned that those first few sentences would lead to a 15-year writing career that has spawned over 20 books under the Robert Kennedy Publishing umbrella. Therefore it shouldn't come as a surprise that I begin by thanking the man himself. Bob's energy, support and leadership are boundless, and I certainly couldn't have completed this book without his inspiration. Thanks Bob.

I'd also like to thank Wendy Morley and her staff at Robert Kennedy Publishing for their expertise and hard work. As always I'm indebted to them for their patience, guidance and skillful manipulation.

Finally to my wife Christine I'd like to say thanks for all her love, support and encouragement. A more wonderful partner and friend I couldn't hope to find.

— Gerard Thorne

Few could argue that bodybuilding is an amazing sport. It has changed and continues to change the lives of millions the world over. Few physical activities provide the same degree of control over your body, allowing you to sculpt it to be exactly what you want it to be.

In the simplest sense bodybuilding is the process of exercising with weights with the two primary purposes of enlarging the muscles and reducing body-fat percentage. Unfortunately this definition omits all the other aspects that make this activity such a positive and rewarding experience. Bodybuilding isn't solely about getting huge; it's about boosting your self-confidence and developing determination. It's about the camaraderie you share with your fellow bodybuilders and "iron pumpers." For some it's the thrill of competition, going mano a mano on stage against other bodybuilders in front of hundreds of people and being rewarded with acclamation of being the best up there. And still for others it's the difference between a healthy life and an early death.

Yes bodybuilding, when you boil it right down, is pretty straightforward:
- Work out
- Follow a sound nutritional program
- Get adequate rest
- Do it all over again
- Grow!

Piece of cake, right? Well not exactly. Our bodies can be stubborn and it will take great discipline, time and dedication for you to achieve the results you want from your training. Further, the bigger you get, the harder it becomes to gain additional muscular body weight. Eventually you will reach a point where gaining even a pound of new muscle tissue in one year is difficult. If you are lacking in only one area (even poor

INTRODUCTION

sleeping habits or inadequate water intake) then your chances of making progress at this point are very much reduced. It is a lot easier to *talk* body-building than actually *do* it!

The purpose of this training manual is to present as much information as possible so you can achieve the results you want in the shortest time possible. I have divided your training into three training phases spread over one year. Everything is there for you – exercises, sets and reps. Each training chapter will also include a section on supple-ments. You may want to read all the supplement sections in one go rather than month by month.

Given its importance, I have devoted an entire chapter to nutrition. You may be following the greatest exercise rou-tine in the world, but if you're not eating the way you should be then don't expect to make serious gains. Five minutes of lousy eating can undermine a whole week's worth of training. If you don't get your eating habits under control you'll be just another "smooth" beefy-looking guy. Worse, you'll be a candidate for cardiovascular disease when you hit your 40s or 50s.

Of course the real challenge for you is to take that knowledge and apply it to your training and diet over the long term. You must make bodybuilding a part of your life and train consistently for months and years at a time. All of the top pro bodybuilders took many years to get as big and as muscular as they are now. But don't let this put you off. With the right combination of ded-ication and perseverance you will ob-tain the results you want and continue to improve, year after year.

— Gerard Thorne

Photo by Paul Buceta
Model Essa Obaid

Photo by Robert Reiff
Model David Hoffman

Photo by Robert Reiff
Model Con Demetriou

Photo by Gregory James
Model Evgeni Mishin

LAYING THE GROUNDWORK

1

CH.
1

LAYING THE GROUNDWORK

While you might think muscle growth results from simply lifting as much weight as you can as many times per week as possible, the reality is much more complex. As with many sports, bodybuilding should be approached logically and with calculation. You want to systematically plan your training sessions so you're not wasting time in the gym. You also want to structure your diet so your body is properly fueled and operating efficiently to promote recovery and muscular gains. With the right balance of mass- and strength-building workouts along with a nutrition plan that supports muscle growth, you can achieve maximum potential with your physique.

PERIODIZATION: TIME MANAGEMENT AT ITS FINEST

Most bodybuilders don't train the same way year round; instead they cycle, or periodize, their training in order to address specific goals and encourage continued progress. During a bulking phase (which is often part of the offseason) many athletes train with heavier weights, doing fewer sets and reps as a strategy to add mass to their frames. When bodybuilders want to lean out (i.e., during the precontest period, for a photo shoot), they'll go through a cutting phase, switching up training variables such as exercises, order, set-and-rep combinations, weight and amount of cardio to drop their bodyfat levels and bring out muscularity.

When you're planning your training program, you need to account for individual factors like genetics and body type, along with the fact that no single method will be continuously effective. Your body is highly adaptable and will get accustomed to your workouts the longer you perform the same routine. As your muscles become familiar with the exercises, weight loads, sets and reps, your progress will begin to slow and eventually come to a halt. To avoid a plateau with your training and instead help ensure ongoing

Building your dream physique is a lot like chasing any other dream. You need to create a logical long-term plan and stick to it.

progress, the general recommendation is to vary your training strategies every six to eight weeks, as doing so within this time frame will keep your body stimulated in different ways.

FREQUENCY OPTIONS

Part of the periodization approach involves changing workout variables such as number of sets and repetitions, time between sets and the exercises you perform to produce the best possible gains in muscle mass and strength. Before outlining the specific workout programs, however, it's important to look first at the various frequency training options.

FULL BODY

One very basic training program is the full-body workout, in which you train all the body's major muscles during the same workout on Day 1, followed by rest on Day 2. You then repeat the session (or similar exercises) on Day 3, rest on Day 4 and do another full-body workout on Day 5. Many individuals structure their gym schedules around the work week, so the most popular way of incorporating such a training program into the week is to train on Monday, Wednesday and Friday, and take Tuesday, Thursday and weekends off. Of course, there's no reason you can't adjust the split to dif-

Photo by Michael Butler
Model Johnnie Jackson

To ensure maximum muscle stimulation, you must vary your training schedule by changing such things as your sets, reps and exercises.

ferent days of the week, depending on what best suits your schedule.

Here are some important points to consider if you want to reap the most benefits of full-body training:

- Train on nonconsecutive days. It takes your body at least 48 hours to recover from a workout, so you'll need a day of rest between each training day.
- Perform only one exercise per muscle group. Because you'll be training your entire body, you'll have enough energy reserves to hit each muscle with only one exercise. Trying to include more movements could put you at risk of overtraining.
  - Use different exercises for each bodypart from one workout to the next to keep your body guessing. For example, if you performed barbell bench presses for your chest on Monday, do incline dumbbell chest presses on Wednesday. By choosing varying exercises each training session, you'll hit the muscles from slightly different angles to promote better overall strength and development. (It's also a good way to keep your workouts interesting!)
- Do just three sets per exercise. You may think the more sets the better, but you have to keep in mind that you're doing three sets of six to eight exercises. In total, that's 18 to 24 sets for one workout, which will place a large demand on your recovery system. Remember, your goal is intensity, not volume.
  - Prioritize compound exercises in your workouts. These movements target two or more muscle groups, whereas isolation moves recruit just one muscle group. Compound exercises will produce greater gains in strength and size than

isolation movements because a higher number of muscle fibers are activated. Examples of very effective compound moves include squats, deadlifts, bench presses and rows.

- Limit your use of weight machines, as most machines isolate muscle groups. Your goal is to use compound exercises that bring in more than one muscle group at a time. While a certain few machines help you get the maximum benefits of the full-body workout, you'll want to concentrate on free weights – equipment like dumbbells and barbells – along with some bodyweight exercises such as pull-ups (chin-ups), push-ups, parallel bars for dips and some abdominal movements.

• Choose a weight that allows you to complete 8 to 10 reps per set. In general, this rep range is ideal for those who want to make size and strength gains using heavy weight. Fewer reps may build more strength, but they don't produce the same degree of muscle hypertrophy (a precursor for growth). Likewise, higher reps (12 or more) tend to be better for conditioning the muscle for better endurance.

"Use different exercises for each bodypart from one workout to the next to keep your body guessing."

• Be mindful of your exercise order. Since full-body workouts target all your major muscle groups, you'll need to pay attention to the order in which you perform the moves. For example, you generally want to avoid working smaller bodyparts such as triceps and biceps early in your workout, as you'll rely heavily on them to assist with your larger chest, back and shoulder exercises. If you perform triceps or biceps movements first, the smaller muscles will be fatigued, limiting the amount of weight you can lift during exercises for the larger muscle groups.

It's also important to perform abdominal and lower-back work (such as back extensions) after you've completed heavier leg exercises such as squats or deadlifts. Both of these big lifts require a great deal of core stability, so if your ab and lumbar muscles are already fatigued, you won't be as strong and may sacrifice proper form on the leg exercises. When your core muscles are tired and you try to perform heavy lower-body work, you put

yourself at an increased risk of injury – the ligaments of the lower back are less forgiving when they have to bear the brunt of the weight.

SPLIT ROUTINES

Training programs that involve a bodypart split have, for the most part, become the standard in bodybuilding. This setup involves separating your workouts by main muscle groups or bodypart and then scheduling one or more areas to target on specific days of the split. Routines can be arranged in many different ways depending on how you respond to training, your overall schedule and your specific physique goals or any lagging bodyparts you want to bring up to par. Here are a few examples of the many versions of split routines.

Three-Day Split

The three-day split is one of the most basic routines of this type. You divide the body's muscle groups among three different workouts and perform each once per week with a rest day between each training day. Here's an example of what a three-day split might look like.

DAY	BODYPARTS TRAINED
1	Chest, back
2	Off
3	Legs, abs
4	Off
5	Shoulders, arms
6	Off

This training format allows ample time for recuperation, as each main muscle group is hit only once every seven days. This split is ideal for bodybuilders who need more recovery days between workouts for the same muscle groups.

Photo by Jason Breeze
Model Lou Joseph

If you're like most people, you have various commitments that may impact on your training availability. But there are ways to arrange a four-day split to work with your life.

Four-Day Split

This training schedule involves separating the body's muscles into two different workouts and then alternating between each, with one rest day falling after two consecutive training days. There are a few different approaches to the four-day split. Here's an example of one option – you train three main bodyparts on Day 1, the other three on Day 2 and then take a day off before repeating the schedule.

DAY	BODYPARTS TRAINED
1	Chest, back, shoulders
2	Legs, arms, abs
3	Off
4	Repeat Day 1
5	Repeat Day 2
6	Off

For some bodybuilders, a main disadvantage of this split is that it doesn't take into account the seven-day week most people structure their lives around with a five-day work week and a two-day weekend. Following this split would mean that over a two-week period you'd be in the gym at least once on all seven days of the week. Commitments such as work, family, school or household responsibilities may impact when you can schedule your training days, and for some individuals, weekends are not an option for working out. Therefore, another version of the four-day split may better suit your lifestyle. Here's a second option – it's similar to the first example, but you also get weekends as off days.

DAY	BODYPARTS TRAINED
1	Chest, back, shoulders
2	Legs, arms, abs
3	Off
4	Repeat Day 1
5	Repeat Day 2
6	Off
7	Off

The four-day split provides balance to your overall program because you hit the muscles hard enough to induce growth without taxing the recovery system too severely (you get three full days' rest out of seven). If you still find three days of rest is not adequate enough (or you can only get to the gym three days a week but still want to follow a split routine) there is yet another variation of the four-day split called the two-week split. With this version you train three times per week, performing Day 1 twice and Day 2 once. Then the following week you'll start with Day 2, so you'll complete that workout twice and Day 1 once. Here's what the two weeks would look like using the two-week split variation.

WEEK 1	
Monday	Day 1
Tuesday	Off
Wednesday	Day 2
Thursday	Off
Friday	Day 1
Saturday	Off
Sunday	Off

WEEK 2	
Monday	Day 2
Tuesday	Off
Wednesday	Day 1
Thursday	Off
Friday	Day 2
Saturday	Off
Sunday	Off

A four-day training split generally allows you to stimulate your muscles into growth without overtaxing your recovery system.

Five-Day Split

This format has become one of the more common training splits used by bodybuilders looking to add impressive muscle mass. Some of the sport's experts, including Charles Poliquin, are big advocates of the five-day split and widely recommend it to their clients. The greatest benefit of this split is that it allows you to train at a much higher intensity level in each workout since each muscle group is hit only once a week.

Here are some options for arranging a five-day split:

- Two days on/one day off/two days on/one day off/one day on
- Three days on/one day off/two days on/one day off
- Three days on/one day off/one day on/one day off/one day on

When choosing the exact breakdown to follow, consider your individual recovery needs as well as your weekly schedule outside the gym.

For a truly intense experience, you can't go wrong with the five-day split. It works each muscle group once a week.

Photo by Gregory James
Model Marcus Haley

The six-day split is so rigorous that even competitive bodybuilders generally limit their use of it to only the precontest phase.

Photo by Alex Ardenti
Models Kai Greene, Jay Cutler and Dexter Jackson

Six-Day Split

This split is a very rigorous training schedule and is recommended only for advanced trainers. There are two ways this split can be arranged. Some bodybuilders break their training into six different workouts and perform each one, once per week. The other version is to do three different workouts, twice per week. The advantage of the former is that it allows a full week between training the same muscle groups, so it can benefit those with slower recovery systems. Bodybuilders who find their muscles recuperate more quickly however, may do well with the latter format. Again, it all comes down to what works best for your individual body and personal training goals.

It's important to remember that six-day splits are not for everyone. You're training different muscle groups each day, but your body is being taxed six out of seven days per week. This level of training could lead many athletes into a state of overtraining. Most bodybuilders limit six-day training to the precontest phase, lasting 10 to 12 weeks, when they want to get as lean and ripped as possible.

Photo by Gregory James
Model Troy Alves

Photo by Paul Buceta
Model Adam Headland

Photo by Robert Reiff
Model Dan Decker

Photo by Rich Baker
Model Tricky Jackson

MUSCLE-BUILDING NUTRITION AND CLEAN EATING

2

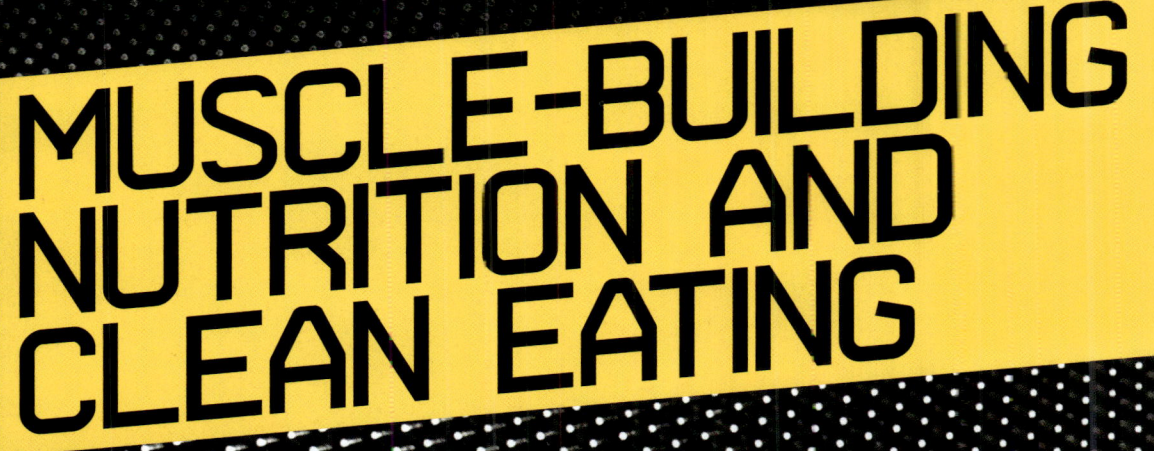

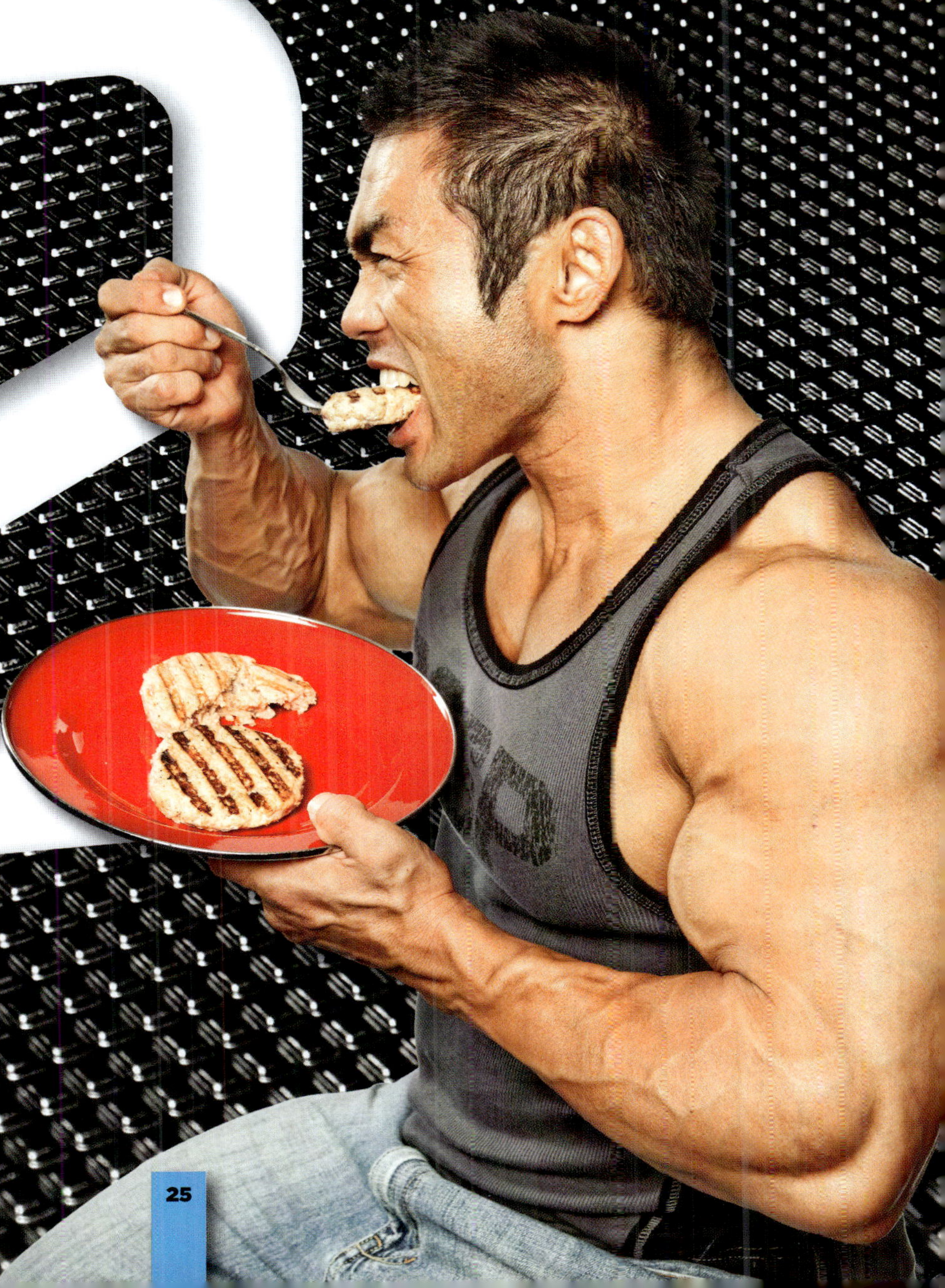

Photo by Robert Reiff
Model Hidetada Yamagishi

CH. 2

MUSCLE-BUILDING NUTRITION AND CLEAN EATING

The late Vince Gironda, bodybuilding and training guru, argued that bodybuilding was 90% nutrition. While some people thought Vince's theories on training and nutrition were unorthodox, his views on the importance of nutrition were right on target. You can't expect to make significant gains in size and strength if you're fueling your body with junk food. Your overall meal plan should be focused on high-quality food sources that contain a wealth of muscle-building and energy-producing nutrients. Your body needs an appropriate balance of the three macronutrients – protein, carbs and fats – along with key micronutrients to carry out all the functions necessary for growth, tissue repair, hormone production, energy, fat burning, metabolism and absorption.

NOT JUST FOR SHOW

A lot of bodybuilders are mainly concerned with nutrition from a muscle-building standpoint (i.e., their main focus is taking in appropriate ratios of protein, carbs and healthy fats to support their efforts in the gym). It's also important to remember, however, that the food choices you make will impact your long-term overall health. Your body requires certain amounts of vitamins, minerals and nutrients to function properly; if your diet is lacking, you may be at increased risk of developing a wide range of health problems. Conditions ranging from cardiovascular disease and stroke to high blood cholesterol levels and diabetes are heavily influenced by your eating habits. Paying attention to your diet, eating healthy foods and breaking poor nutrition habits will put you on the right track toward long-term wellness. When you're thinking about your physique goals, keep in mind that your muscles are only part of the equation. You need every system in your body working at full capacity in order to reach and maintain your maximum physical potential. Part of bodybuilding includes the pursuit of ongoing good health, so you have to

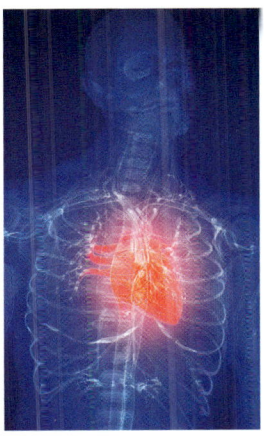

To make the most of your training efforts and sculpt the physique of your dreams, you'll need to focus on your diet.

make a determined effort to incorporate and follow proper eating habits.

MACRONUTRIENT GROUPS

Protein

Protein is the general term for molecules made up of linear chains of amino acids. Your body uses approximately 22 amino acids (though scientists disagree on this number; some data notes 20 in total and other experts argue anywhere from 24 to 28 amino acids exist). Amino acids can link up in a variety of sequences to create different types of protein. The core functions of protein include providing material for building muscle tissue, producing cells and hormones, fighting infection, producing enzymes and facilitating neurotransmitter activity.

Quality Food Sources: Skinless chicken breast, skinless turkey breast, lean red meat, lean pork, egg whites, tuna, salmon, trout, herring, white fish, skim or low-fat milk products, lentils and beans.

Carbohydrates

Carbohydrates are the primary fuel source for the human body. They are grouped as sugars, starches, celluloses and gums. Carbohydrates are divided into two subgroups, digestible (dietary carbs) and indigestible (fibrous carbs or dietary fiber). Individuals who exercise regularly need adequate amounts of carbohydrates in their systems as an available energy source. When you're trying to build muscle mass, it's even more crucial to take in ample carbohydrates, not only for the energy concerns but also to regulate the conversion of protein into new muscle tissue. Without enough carbs (or with the wrong type of carbs), your body will start looking elsewhere for fuel and end up burning muscle tissue.

Digestible carbohydrates can be categorized into two primary subgroups: simple carbs and complex carbs. Simple carbohydrates, or sugars, are absorbed quickly by the body, while complex carbohydrates take more time to digest. Simple carbs are more likely to get stored as fat since they get converted to glucose and thus cause a rapid increase in the body's primary storage hormone, insulin. Examples of this carb form include white-flour products, fruit juice, jam, honey and maple syrup. Aside from the post-workout period when your body can make good use of the fast-digesting type, try to consume most of your carbohydrates

If you're looking to build an impressive physique, a well-balanced diet is essential, as it'll provide the fuel necessary to stimulate your gains.

Photo by Robert Reiff
Model Binais Begovic

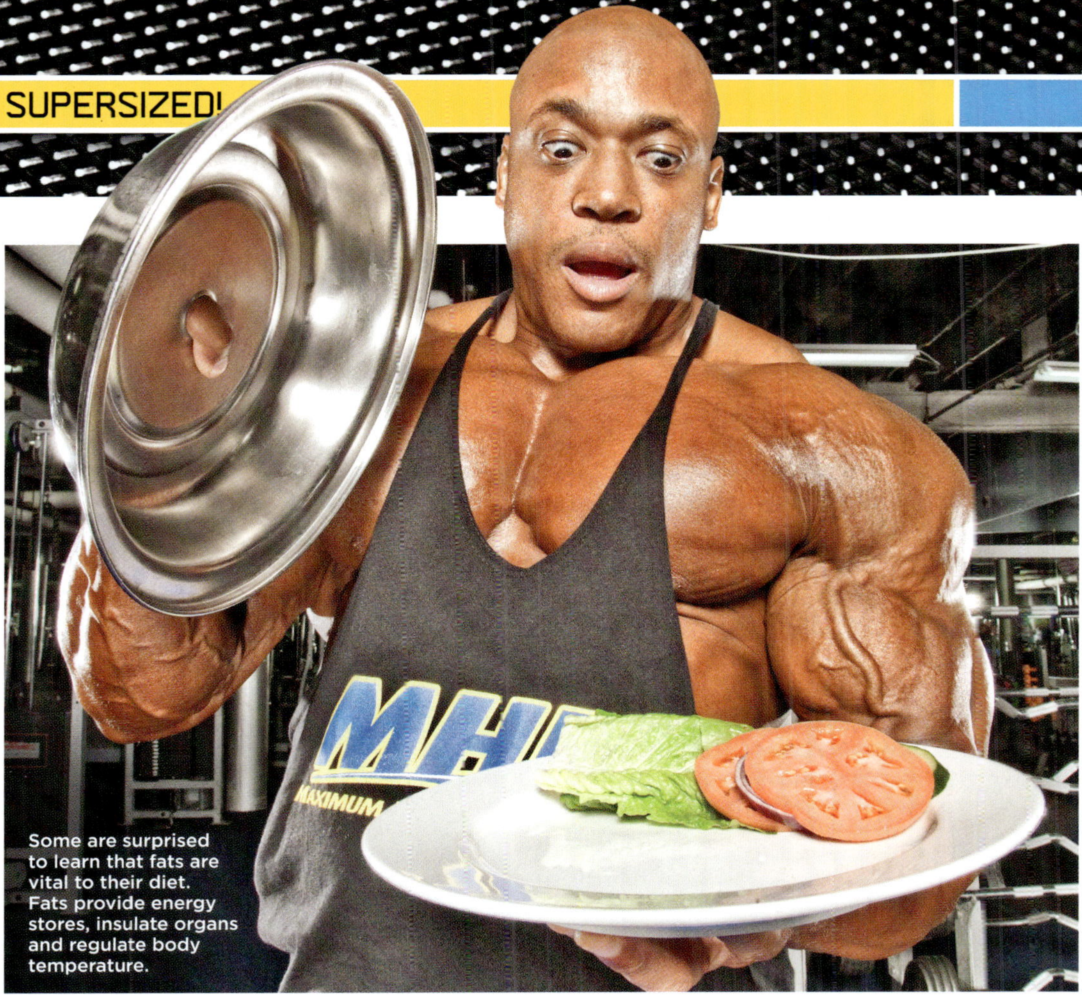

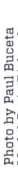

Some are surprised to learn that fats are vital to their diet. Fats provide energy stores, insulate organs and regulate body temperature.

from complex sources. Whole foods of this form include whole-grain bread and pasta products, oats, sweet potato, brown rice and legumes.

Fats and Oils

Fats are a vast group of compounds and can be either solid (butter) or liquid (oil) at room temperature. Dietary sources of fat get broken down into fatty acids in the body. Many individuals incorrectly assume that all fat is bad, but this macronutrient has many vital physiological roles such as infusing the body with essential fatty acids, providing energy stores, insulating organs, promoting healthy cell function and regulating body temperature. Fats also transport fat-soluble vitamins and are responsible for male hormone production.

Three primary types of fats exist naturally: saturated, monounsaturated and polyunsaturated. Saturated fats are usually solid at room temperature and they're the form most likely to cause the buildup of plaque in your arteries and raise your LDL ("bad") cholesterol. Individuals whose diets are high in this form of fat are at higher risk for developing atherosclerosis and coronary heart disease. Because of the associated health risks, you should limit consumption of this type of fat – daily intake should be less than 10% of total calories. However saturated fat is important for testosterone production, so don't cut it out completely (and it would be difficult to eliminate all saturated fat if you consume animal products). Common sources include animal fats such as beef, poultry, lard, full-fat dairy products and butter along with plant sources such as coconut oil and palm oil.

Photo by Paul Buceta
Model Craig Richardson

Polyunsaturated fats provide linolenic and linoleic acid, part of the omega-3 and omega-6 families of fatty acids, respectively, which are essential for health. This type of fat can be found in fatty fish such as salmon, sardines and mackerel along with oils such as flax, safflower and canola. Even though there are many benefits associated with this type of fat (e.g., it reduces blood clotting, lowers blood pressure, prevents irregular heartbeat, lowers triglycerides), you should still limit your intake to approximately 10% of total calories per day.

Monounsaturated fats are termed the "good" fats because they increase your level of HDLs and lower your LDLs. This form should make up the greatest portion of your total fat intake. Monounsaturated oils such as olive (a staple of the Mediterranean diet) have been shown

> "Many individuals incorrectly assume that all fat is bad, but this macronutrient has many vital physiological roles."

to offer a wealth of physical benefits including heart health. Other quality sources of this form of fat include all varieties of nuts as well as avocados.

Trans Fat

Trans fat doesn't occur naturally in foods but rather is the result of 20th-century food-processing techniques. While the technological advances in the food industry have greatly answered the need for mass food production, they have introduced a new set of health concerns including the negative effects of trans fat in the body.

Trans fat is a product of 20th century advancements that should be avoided. Choose healthier, fresher foods and your body will flourish.

During processing, hydrogen atoms are added to natural fats and oils through a series of steps to make them creamier, more solid and to increase shelf life. However, the human body lacks any enzymes to process trans fat. Instead, it ends up in the liver where it's either stored or returned to the bloodstream and deposited in fat cells. Any time you read hydrogenated/partially hydrogenated vegetable oil or shortening on ingredient labels, it means the product contains trans fat. You should try to avoid items containing trans fat as much as possible and look for more healthful alternatives.

Photo by Robert Reiff
Model Ben Pakulski

Photo by Paul Buceta
Model Fouad Abiad

31

Micronutrients – Vitamins and Minerals

Vitamins and minerals are organic and inorganic substances your body needs in very small amounts for growth, repair, various bodily functions and general maintenance of good health. Most of your micronutrient requirements can be met via diet, but if you don't get enough variety in the foods you eat regularly, you may risk a deficiency in one or more micronutrients. Certain food sources have more vitamins and minerals than others, so it's important to eat a well-balanced diet that includes a wide range of items from all the food groups.

> "Some bodybuilders opt to take a daily multivitamin supplement, but the reality is that consuming a well-balanced diet will help ensure all your basic needs are fully met."

Vitamins

Vitamins are organic substances that fall into two general categories: fat-soluble and water-soluble. Vitamins A, D, E and K are classified as fat-soluble because they dissolve and can be stored in the body's fat, so your body can tap into the stores when necessary. Water-soluble vitamins, which include C and the B-complex vitamins, can't be stored in the body. Any excess amount your body doesn't use gets excreted in your urine.

Minerals

Minerals are inorganic elements that come from soil and water and then get absorbed by plants or eaten by animals.

Photo by Gary Bartlett
Models Ronny Rockel, Jay Cutler, Phil Heath, Branch Warren and Dexter Jackson

Your body needs the full spectrum of minerals in various amounts to grow and maintain health. The minerals your body requires in larger amounts, such as calcium, are called macrominerals, whereas other minerals such as chromium, copper, iodine, iron, selenium and zinc are called trace minerals because you need them only in very small amounts each day.

The best way to get all the vitamins and minerals your body requires for proper function is to eat a wide variety of sources from each food group. Your bodybuilding meal plan should consist mainly of whole, unprocessed food sources such as lean meats, fish, poultry, fresh fruits and vegetables, whole grains and low-fat dairy products. Some bodybuilders opt to take a daily multivitamin supplement, but the reality is that consuming a well-balanced diet will help ensure all your basic needs are fully met.

Photo by Robert Reiff
Model Tony Breznik

Vitamins and minerals are a vital part of every successful bodybuilder's diet. They help maintain overall good health and are essential to muscle growth.

Photo by Gregory James
Model Troy Alves

Photo by Rich Baker
Model Tim Liggins

Photo by Rich Baker
Model Johnnie Jackson

Photo by Paul Buceta
Model Ahmad Haidar

POST-WORKOUT NUTRITION

POST-WORKOUT NUTRITION

Serious bodybuilders know that both the pre- and post-workout periods are critical times for nutrition. Some experts in the sport argue that the meal you consume after training is the most important of the day, as your body is depleted and needs specific amounts of nutrients to recover and grow. Without proper nutrition during the post-workout window, you risk slipping into a state of catabolism (muscle-wasting) because your body won't get enough fuel to replace what was lost during training. Post-workout nutrition doesn't have to be complicated; you just need to know the basics of which nutrients your body does and doesn't need, and what the best sources are.

DOS AND DON'TS OF POST-WORKOUT NUTRITION

During the post-workout period your body needs two primary nutrients: protein and carbs, mainly fast-digesting carbs. You should try to avoid high-fat foods after training because fat has one characteristic that makes it a poor choice for post-workout nutrition – it slows digestion. More specifically, it interferes with digestion of the two main nutrients you do need, protein and simple carbs.

PROTEIN

The building material of the body, protein makes up most of the body's structures and organs, including the muscles. Since this macronutrient can be found in various forms (amino acids link together in many different sequences to create a variety of complete and incomplete proteins), you want to choose specific food sources that will give you the best protein form for the post-workout period.

When you consume protein immediately after a workout, you want a source that digests quickly to send amino acids into your bloodstream. Certain protein sources, however, aren't ideal after training because they don't get absorbed fast enough to feed muscle tissue and prevent breakdown. Whole-food proteins such as egg whites, chicken and tuna are great sources

To avoid catabolism following a muscle-building workout, you'll need to eat foods rich in protein and fast-digesting simple carbs.

of protein that you should be including regularly in your bodybuilding diet, but they digest more slowly and thus aren't the optimal type of protein for your post-workout meal.

The problem with consuming whole foods after training is the very fact that they're whole. The body takes extra

> "Without proper nutrition during the post-workout window, you risk slipping into a state of catabolism (muscle wasting)."

time to break them down before the nutrients can be absorbed. If you eat a high-protein whole-food meal after your workout, a considerable amount of time will pass before the protein is digested and becomes ready for your body to use. For the most benefit, you should be consuming fast-digesting nutrients within the first hour of completing your training session. There-

fore, you want to choose a high-protein source that's easy to eat and digest, and combine it with a fast-digesting carb source to help shuttle nutrients into your cells and tissues. Whey protein powder fits the bill as an ideal source of protein to eat after your workout.

Whey protein is one of the fastest-digesting protein sources available, making it a top choice at such a critical time post workout. And because you will consume this protein as a liquid once you mix it into a shake, your body won't have to work hard to break it down, so you will be able to digest the nutrients much more quickly. In general, you should try to take in approximately 1.0 to 1.5 grams of protein per pound of bodyweight per day. If you're eating six meals per day and spreading your protein intake evenly, your post-workout shake should contain roughly 0.15 to 0.25 grams of protein per pound of bodyweight. A 200-pound bodybuilder, for example, should consume 30 to 50 grams of protein post workout. Most whey protein powders on the market come with a premeasured scoop. One scoop usually equates to about 20 grams of protein. Just be sure to check the label on the protein powder you use, as it will give you a precise breakdown of the nutrients per serving and the size of that serving.

CARBS

After training, your body also needs adequate amounts of carbohydrates to restore muscle glycogen levels, replenish energy stores and help amino acids move into the bloodstream. If your post workout meal doesn't contain adequate amounts of carbohydrates, specifically in the simple form, your body may start to break down muscle tissue for energy purposes.

One of the best ways to refuel following a workout is with a refreshing protein shake. Add a fruit for flavor and carbs.

Dextrose is a favorite drink among bodybuilders because of its well-known ability to be quickly absorbed into the bloodstream

Another main function carbohydrates serve after training is to increase the release of insulin. As one of your body's primary storage hormones, insulin speeds the transport of nutrients including protein into the bloodstream and throughout the body.

While your overall diet should strongly favor complex over simple carbohydrates, post-workout is the one time of day when you should consume the simple form. Complex carbs such as wholewheat bread and brown rice contain more fiber, which slows their digestion

considerably. Conversely, high-glycemic, simple carbs elevate blood sugar rapidly and spike insulin levels to help drive nutrients into your muscle cells. A popular post-workout carbohydrate choice among bodybuilders is dextrose, which is glucose that's been derived from corn. It can be absorbed directly through the gut into the bloodstream because it's already in the form your body requires. The general recommendation for dextrose consumption post workout is in the range of 0.25 to 0.4 grams per pound of bodyweight. Again, follow the label

Photos by Rich Baker
Models Ruben Justiniano / Steve Namat

The first 45 minutes following a workout is a very important time. It's during this time that your body soaks up nutrients like a sponge.

directions for appropriate serving size. You can also get your post-workout carbs from fruit, which can be conveniently added to your protein shake.

TIMING

After a workout, your body is like a nutrient sponge. Research shows the body absorbs and utilizes nutrients during the first 45 minutes post workout at a far greater capacity than any other time. This "post-workout window" continues to a lesser degree up to 90 minutes after training. To reap the most benefits, how-ever, you should aim to consume your shake within 45 minutes. During the post-workout window, the two main nutrient sources your body needs are fast-digesting protein and simple carbs to replenish energy stores, promote muscle growth and facilitate recovery. One of the easiest ways to feed your muscles in the shortest time possible is to have your post-workout shake ingredients handy in your gym bag. Then, as soon as you've completed your training session, you can simply mix everything in a shaker cup and it's ready to drink immediately.

Photo by Gregory James
Model Joao Câneco

Photo by Robert Reiff
Model Binais Begovic

Photo by Gregory James
Model Tad Inoue

Photo by Rich Baker
Model Brian Yersky

OVERTRAINING

Photo by Gregory James
Model: Mhora Edwards

43

CH.
4

OVERTRAINING

Many individuals

struggle with negative health effects associated with a lack of exercise, but while it may not be as common, excessive or extreme training has the same potential to damage your body. Bodybuilders and athletes are prone to the condition known as overtraining because of their strict workout schedules, the high physical demands associated with sport and the emphasis on performance.

Exercise physiologists use the term overtraining to describe the state that occurs when you train your body too frequently, with too much intensity or without enough recovery time. Some bodybuilders push themselves beyond reasonable limits in the gym with the mindset that more work will lead to better results. The truth is, your body can cope with only a certain level of stress from exercise before it starts to respond poorly and progress comes to a halt. In order to add muscle and strength, your body must be in an anabolic state, but overtraining causes the body to slip into a state of catabolism, or muscle wasting, so you can actually lose muscle mass. A number of secondary factors can contribute to overtraining, such as an inadequate

nutrition plan, poor sleeping habits, an insufficient supplement regimen and underlying health issues, but training is the primary influence. Therefore, it's important to be very conscious of all aspects of your workout program including the bodypart split, intensity, volume, exercises performed, set-and-rep schemes and amount of cardio versus weights. If you push yourself hard at the gym almost every day of the week, you may not be giving your muscles or nervous system enough time to recover between workouts. Eventually your body will reach a point where training and performance become impaired, energy level decreases and muscle gains either plateau or even start to reverse. Recovery from a truly overtrained state may take anywhere from a couple of weeks to as much as a few months.

A lot of bodybuilders may discredit the idea of overtraining, but doing so is a mistake. Overtraining leads to a loss in muscle mass.

Photo by Robert Reiff
Model David Hughes

If your muscles and joints are aching your body may be trying to tell you that you're overtraining.

attention to how your body reacts. A training journal can be a very useful tool to help you track the specifics of your workouts along with how you felt before, during and after. You can also see how your body reacts over the long term. With detailed notes, you will have a quick reference of what works for you and what doesn't. The routines outlined in *Supersized!* have been designed to gradually increase the intensity of your training. As your body begins to adapt, the routines progress to challenge your muscles in more vigorous ways and encourage continued growth. Because every bodybuilder is different, however, small adjustments to the workouts may be necessary, depending on how you respond. If you're struggling to keep up with any aspect of the routines such as the number of workouts per week, exercise volume or sets and reps, you can make minor modifications to ensure that you're training at a suitable level for your physique and that you avoid overtraining.

At any point during the program, if you notice your muscles feel excessively sore, you are constantly tired or your muscular gains have stopped or even regressed, be sure to take a break from hardcore training – start with one week and then judge how you feel after that time period before heading back into the gym to pick up the same routine. Some bodybuilders who have reached an overtrained state need two or three weeks off from serious working out before feeling well enough to return to their programs. Doing just some light exercise during that period can help your body recover. Instead of hitting the weights try engaging in one or two hours of active rest at some point throughout the day. This may involve some light walking or stretching and can also include low-impact activities.

Here are some of the most common symptoms of overtraining:

- Fatigue
- Restless sleep or insomnia
- Halted muscular gains, or a decrease in muscle size or strength levels
- Lack of motivation to train
- Loss of appetite
- Aching muscles and joints
- Difficulty achieving pump when training
- Elevated heart rate upon waking in the morning

PREVENTION AND TREATMENT OF OVERTRAINING

The best ways to avoid slipping into an overtrained state are to carefully plan your training, diet and supplementation programs and then pay very close

Photo by Kevin Horton
Model Rodney Roller and Brian May

If you're experiencing any symptoms of overtraining you should also review your diet plan. Here are some main questions to consider:

- Are you meeting your basic macronutrient needs, with appropriate ratios of protein, carbs and fats?
- Do you eat five or six meals a day, spaced approximately every two to three hours apart?
- Are you consuming 1 to 1.5 grams of protein per pound of bodyweight each day?
- Do the majority of your carbohydrates come from complex sources?
- Does your diet include the right amount of each type of fat?
- Are you getting enough of the proper nutrients during your pre- and post-workout periods?

Addressing your nutrition along with other main factors that impact your progress as a bodybuilder – training program, supplementation, sleep and recovery – can help you pinpoint specific problem areas. You can then make changes as needed to get your body back on track for continued mass building.

Hardcore training leads some bodybuilders into an overtrained state. If you reach that state, you may need to take two to three weeks off.

Photo by Robert Reiff
Model Will Harris

Photo by Rich Baker
Model Andy Haman

Photo by Rich Baker
Model Larry Vinette

Photo by Paul Buceta
Model Michael Kefalianos

THE BEGINNING

THE BEGINNING

At the start of every workout you should spend at least five minutes warming up your entire body. A proper warm-up session will slightly elevate your heart rate and prepare your muscles for the work ahead in your routine. Do some low-impact cardio such as jogging or cycling on a stationary bike, and perform a few movements with light weights. You should include exercises for bodyparts you'll be targeting that day to prime those muscles specifically. Most bodybuilders will do one or two light warm-up sets at the beginning of each new exercise in their training session to individually ready the muscles, tendons and joints for the heavier weight during the working sets. This warm-up approach helps prevent injury.

Over the course of the first three months of this program you'll perform a different routine in each of your three weekly workouts. You'll be hitting all the major muscle groups, but by rotating the exercises you'll be targeting each area from slightly different angles. Slight variations to your training such as this will promote continuous progress and muscular gains. Most of the exercises in this program are compound (also called multijoint), so they involve movement at two or more joints and target several muscles or muscle groups at a time. Because they recruit a high number of muscle fibers, compound exercises are very beneficial for mass and strength building.

During the first month of training, you'll use lighter weights for higher reps, in the range of 12 to 15. Starting off with heavy weight for lower reps would be very stressful on your muscles and joints, and your goal on this program is to make gradual and continual strength improvements and mass gains. Performing a higher-rep/lower-weight routine during this initial phase will provide enough intensity to induce the muscle damage necessary for growth.

Your primary goal during the first month of training should be to learn proper technique on all the exer-

A proper warm-up session is a must. Do a little cardio work and perform a couple of light sets to ready your body

Photo by Rich Baker
Model Con Demetriou

cises. Using good form will decrease your risk of injury and preserve your joints and ligaments while at the same time effectively working your muscles.

After month one, you'll increase the training intensity by increasing the weight and decreasing the rep count to the range of 8 to 12. Then, in month three you'll begin laying the groundwork for the more advanced programs introduced in month four and beyond.

The importance of rep ranges is that they determine the amount of weight you can use. In any given rep range, you want to be working very hard to achieve the last rep. Obviously you would need a smaller weight to work hard at the 12th rep than you would to work hard at the 6th, for example. When you are working within a rep range, say, 8 to 12, you begin with a weight that makes you work for the 8th rep. As you get stronger you will be able to do more reps. Once you can complete 12 reps with ease, you will increase the weight to bring you back

down to 8 reps. So when you read that you should work in a certain rep range, that also tells you the weights you should be using.

MONTH ONE

Weeks 1 and 2: Perform each exercise for three sets of 12 to 15 reps. You will do this full-body workout three times over the week, making sure to leave at least one day between each of your workouts in order for your body to regenerate. Monday, Wednesday and Friday is a typical plan for a three times per week schedule.

DAYS 1, 2 AND 3
Leg Press
Lying Leg Curl
Standing Calf Raise
Flat-Bench Barbell Press
Lat Pulldowns to Front
Dumbbell Front Press
Triceps Pressdown
Barbell Curl
Crunch

Photo by Paul Buceta
Model Tricky Jackson

Week 3: This week you will learn some new exercises for your repertoire, sticking to basic, mostly multijoint choices. You will continue to use weights for reps in the 12 to 15 range.

Week 4: You will learn a few more exercises this week to add some variety to your routine and to work your muscles from different angles, helping stimulate growth.

DAY 1
Squat
Stiff-Legged Deadlift
Seated Calf Raise
Incline Dumbbell Press
Seated Row
Skullcrusher
Alternating Dumbbell Curl
Captain's Chair or Hanging Leg Raise

DAY 2
Leg Press
Lying Leg Curl
Standing Calf Raise
Flat-Bench Barbell Press
Lat Pulldown to Front
Dumbbell Front Press
Triceps Pressdown
Barbell Curl
Crunch

DAY 3
Squat
Stiff-Legged Deadlift
Seated Calf Raise
Incline Dumbbell Press
Seated Row
Skullcrusher
Alternating Dumbbell Curl
Captain's Chair or Hanging Leg Raise

DAY 1
Smith-Machine Squat
Lying Leg Curl
Standing Calf Raise
Flat-Bench Barbell Press
Seated Row
Dumbbell Front Press
Barbell Curl
Skullcrusher
Crunch

DAY 2
Leg Press
Stiff-Legged Deadlift
Toe Press
Incline-Bench Dumbbell Press
Lat Pulldown
Dumbbell Lateral Raise
Preacher Curl
Triceps Pressdown
Leg Raise

DAY 3
Walking Lunge
Seated Leg Curl
Seated Calf Raise
Dip
Barbell Row
Bent-Over Dumbbell Lateral Raise
Standing Dumbbell Curl
Dumbbell Extension
30-Second Plank

Photo by Paul Buceta
Model Loutfi Ajaoun

MONTH TWO

At this point your muscles will have developed enough that you can reduce your rep ranges to 8 to 12 (and therefore increase your weights accordingly). You will still be working out three days a week with full-body workouts. You may be anxious to start different workout splits but you will build more muscle by holding off on more advanced routines until you've developed this base. You will be starting to do more than one exercise for your larger bodyparts, however. Alternate between the following two workouts, so week 1 you will do workout A, workout B, workout A, whereas on week 2 you will do workout B, workout A, workout B. Continue in this manner for four weeks.

WORKOUT A

- Barbell Squat
- Leg Extension
  (do 12 to 15 reps for this exercise)
- Stiff-Legged Deadlift
- Standing Calf Raise
- Seated Calf Raise
- Flat-Bench Barbell Press
- Incline Dumbbell Press
- Seated Row
- Lat Pulldown
- Lateral Raise
- Skullcrusher
- Alternating Dumbbell Curl
- Captain's Chair or Hanging Leg Raise
  (do 12 to 15 reps for this exercise)

WORKOUT B

- Leg Press
- Hack Squat
- Lying Leg Curl
- Standing Calf Raise
- Seated Calf Raise
- Push-Up on Handles
- Pec-Deck
- Barbell Row
- One-Arm Row
- Dumbbell Front Press
- Triceps Dip
- EZ-Bar Curl
- Crunch
  (do 12 to 15 reps for this exercise)

MONTH THREE

This will be your last month of full-body workouts; next month you will begin splitting up your routine. Because you've developed strength now not only in your muscles but also in your tendons and ligaments, you are ready to move to a 6-to-8 rep range. Because of this weight increase you will have to perform a light warm-up set before your work sets. Do one light set of about 15 reps in each bodypart's first exercise, to get your muscles and joints all warmed up. This may seem like a waste of time but it's a much

Photo by Robert Reiff
Model Mike Ergas

greater waste of time to stop training for three months while you rehab an injury. This month you will do the same as last month, rotating between two workouts specifically designed to help you achieve your muscle mass goals.

WORKOUT A

Barbell Squat

Hack Squat

Lying Leg Curl

Standing Calf Raise

Seated Calf Raise

Flat-Bench Press

Cable Crossover
(do 15 to 20 reps for this exercise)

Chin-Up*

One-Arm Cable Row (Lawnmower Pull)

Front Dumbbell Press

Close-Grip Bench Press

Preacher Curl

Reverse Crunch
(do 15 to 20 reps for this exercise)

Twisting Crunch
(do 15 to 20 reps for this exercise)

*If you are unable to do chin-ups, do assisted chin-ups until you can do the real thing. If your gym has an assisted chin-up machine, that's great. Otherwise, place a chair underneath the chin-up bar. Use as much of your bodyweight as possible while lifting, but allow a portion of your weight to remain on the chair or bench. Each time you perform this exercise try to increase the proportion of bodyweight you are lifting.

WORKOUT B

Barbell Deadlift

Stiff-Legged Deadlift

Leg Press

Toe Press

Push-Up on Handles

Chest Dip

Barbell Row

Close-Grip Lat Pulldown

Wide-Grip Upright Row

Skullcrusher

EZ-Bar Curl

Captain's Chair or Hanging Leg Raise
(do 15 to 20 reps for this exercise)

Plank (do 3, holding for at least 30 seconds each time)

Photo by Paul Buceta
Model Manuel Romero

Want to get a greater pump from your workout? Try adding creatine to your supplement regimen and results are sure to follow.

SUPPLEMENTS
Creatine

Since the early 1990s, with mass production and mainstream availability, creatine has become one of the best-selling supplements on the market. A nitrogenous molecule, creatine was actually first identified by French scientist Michel Eugene Chevreul in 1838, but it wasn't until the 1960s that synthetic creatine production began. This is also when athletes in the former Eastern Bloc countries reportedly started using it for power sports including weightlifting and track and field.

Creatine has been widely studied and is strongly supported by credible scientific research. Numerous articles about the effectiveness of creatine have been published in various sports and medical journals, and this supplement has been the topic of many papers presented at various meetings such as the National Strength and Conditioning Association's Creatine Symposium. Creatine is one of the most extensively studied nutritional sports supplements available to athletes.

How it Works

Research indicates that creatine works by increasing production of adenosine triphosphate (ATP) in the body. ATP is the main source of short-term energy (such as you use in weight training), as it transports chemical energy within cells for metabolism. Studies demonstrate that creatine specifically elevates the supply of ATP by increasing the availability of adenosine diphosphate (ADP) molecules, which are then combined with single phosphate ions and converted back to ATP. With more ATP in your body, a greater energy source is

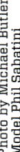
Photo by Michael Butler
Model Phil Sabatini

available to skeletal muscle and therefore more energy for muscle contractions. Scientific evidence indicates that short-term supplementation with creatine effectively boosts creatine concentration in muscles and augments power and performance during workouts.

How to Use

Creatine is naturally synthesized in the liver, pancreas and kidneys from L-arginine, glycine and L-methionine, which are precursor amino acids. About half of the stored creatine in your body comes from food, mainly meat and fish sources. However, most individuals have the physiological capacity to store only 60 to 80 percent of creatine present in the system at any given time. Supplementing with creatine has been shown to improve the body's ability to store creatine by an average of 30 percent. More efficient storage leads to higher concentrations of creatine in muscles. As a result, the body can produce more ATP to provide an increased energy supply to muscles.

Proper dosages for creatine will vary among individuals, but you should be looking for the lowest dose that provides maximum benefit. The general recommendation for oral creatine supplements is to take 5 to 20 grams per day. This amount has been shown in research to increase maximal force production and improve physiological response to exercise with limited adverse side effects. Many bodybuilders opt to use brief loading phases when supplementing with creatine. This strategy involves taking approximately 5 grams of creatine three or four times a day for a period of five to seven days with the purpose of reaching a consistently high serum level of creatine. After loading, bodybuilders will then go through a maintenance phase, which consists of supplementing with 2 to 5 grams per day to sustain the elevated creatine concentration. While loading is a popular supplementation approach with creatine, some health experts suggest the initial loading phase is unnecessary and wasteful because excess creatine the body can't hold just gets excreted. Instead, they recommend starting with the maintenance phase of 2 to 5 grams per day to achieve the same muscle saturation as the individual who loads in two to three weeks.

Absorption of creatine is enhanced when combined with simple sugars such as dextrose that increase insulin levels. Some bodybuilders opt for creatine supplements sold in juice form,

> **"Scientific evidence indicates that short-term supplementation with creatine effectively boosts creatine concentration in muscles and augments power and performance."**

so the products already contain the appropriate fast-digesting carbs to boost absorption. Other athletes prefer to mix their own drinks, adding creatine powder to juice that's high in dextrose (dextrose powder is also used). As part of your supplement regimen, you should take creatine during both the pre- and post-workout periods for best results. Some studies have shown that exercised muscles will absorb more creatine than non-exercised muscles, so the post-workout window is especially crucial. During your off days from the gym, you can still take a low dose of creatine with a carbohydrate meal to maintain muscle stores.

Side Effects

Individual responses to creatine will vary. Creatine appears to be generally safe, according to research, but when taken in high doses there's risk of serious side effects such as kidney damage and the inhibition of the body's natural formation of creatine. Documented side effects of creatine supplementation include weight gain, muscle cramps, muscle strains and pulls, stomach upset, diarrhea, dizziness, high blood pressure, liver dysfunction and kidney damage. Most studies have found no significant adverse effects at the recommended doses used for up to six months.

Some experts have speculated that creatine supplementation can lead to increased injuries. They argue that creatine improves the explosive energy production of muscle cells but doesn't actually fortify the mechanical strength of the muscles and their attached tendons and associated ligaments. Therefore, an imbalance is created and the powerful muscle contractions might cause strains or even tears in the muscles and connective tissues. To the best of my knowledge, however, there is lacking scientific evidence linking the use of creatine supplements to a heightened instance of damage to muscle or connective tissue.

NUTRITION

Throughout this program you should aim to eat five or six meals a day, ideally spaced every two to three hours apart. A good starting point for your intake of macronutrients is a 35:50:15 ratio of protein to carbs to fats. Make minor adjustments as necessary depending on how your body responds to this baseline breakdown. Here's a sample daily meal plan to give you a sense of what you should be consuming to meet your nutrient needs on this program.

Breakfast

- Omelet made with 4–6 egg whites, 1 whole egg, ¼ cup fat-free cheese and 1 cup vegetables (e.g., mushrooms, onions, green peppers, tomatoes), olive oil cooking spray
- 1 cup 100% fruit juice
- 1 cup steel-cut oats, cooked

Mid-Morning Snack

- Protein shake prepared with 1–2 scoops whey protein powder, water (or low-fat/nonfat milk)
- 1 banana

Lunch

- Tuna salsa wrap prepared with 1 (6-ounce) can of tuna, 1 large (or 2 small) whole-wheat tortilla, ¼ cup salsa, 1 cup lettuce (shredded), 1 tbsp. fat-free mayonnaise
- ¼ cup almonds

Mid-Afternoon Snack

- Protein shake prepared with 1–2 scoops whey protein powder (approximately 20–40 grams of protein), water (or low-fat/nonfat milk)

Dinner

- 8 ounces boneless, skinless chicken breast or salmon fillet, grilled
- 1 cup brown rice (cooked measurement)
- 1 cup mixed vegetables

Before-Bed Snack

- Protein shake prepared with 1 scoop (approximately 25 grams of protein) casein protein powder, water (or low-fat/nonfat milk)

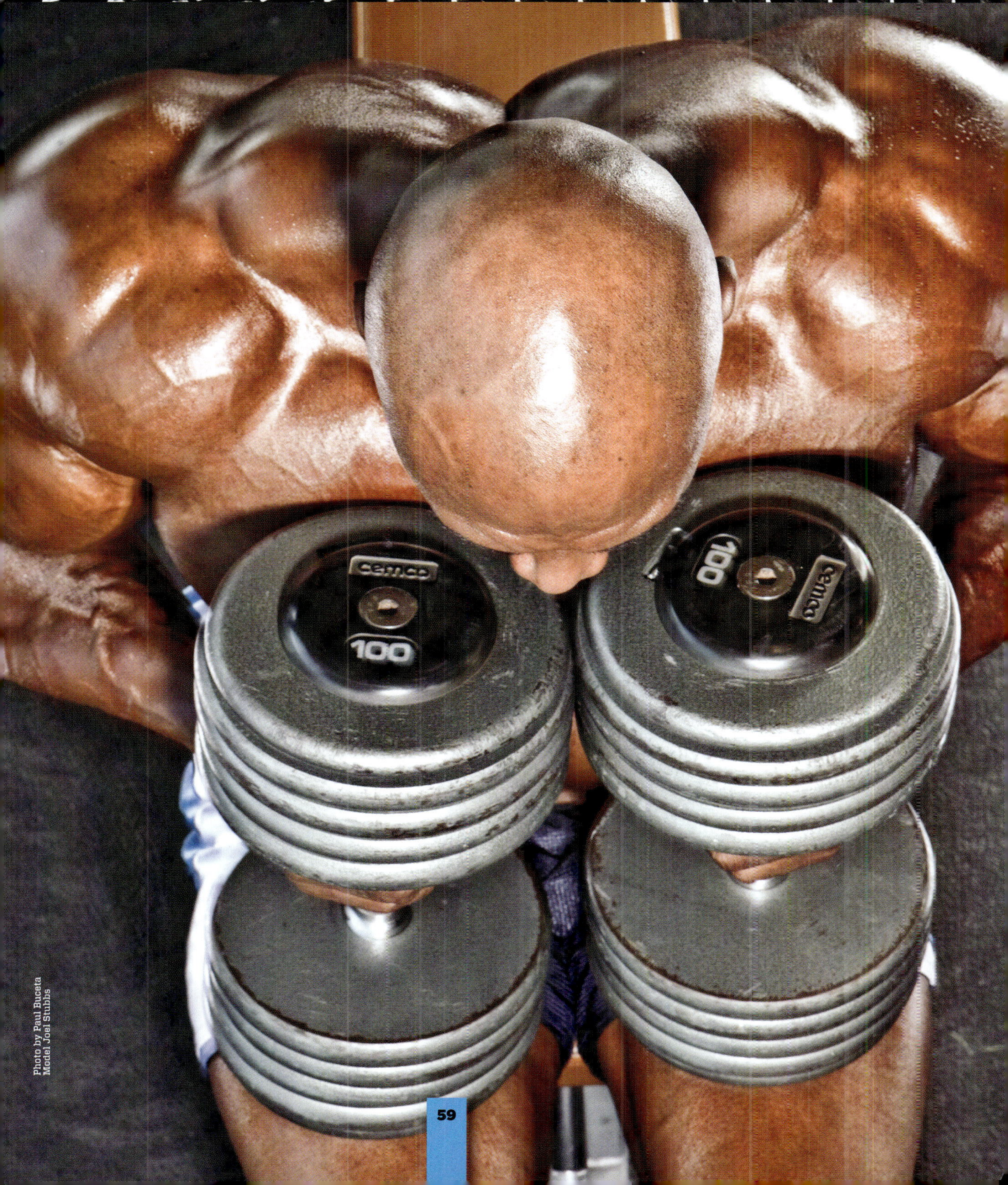

Photo by Paul Buceta
Model Joel Stubbs

Photo by Paul Buceta
Model Santana Anderson

Photo by Robert Reiff
Model Mike O'Hearn

Photo by Jason Breeze
Model Darrem Charles

Photo by Gregory James
Model Marcus Haley

FOUR-DAY TRAINING SPLIT

CH.
6

FOUR-DAY TRAINING SPLIT

At this point in the program your strength levels will have improved and your muscles will be better conditioned to perform a more intense routine. You are now an intermediate bodybuilder and your muscles, tendons and ligaments will be able to handle more work. The core of your workouts will still include basic compound exercises, but this month you'll start adding some isolation exercises. You'll perform two different workouts, doing each one twice per week.

For month four you'll follow a two-days-on/one-day-off, two-days-on/two-days-off split. You'll perform one of the workouts on Monday and Thursday and the other on Tuesday and Friday. Wednesday, Saturday and Sunday are off days. This split can be adjusted to better fit your schedule as long as you're doing each workout twice per week, you're leaving at least 48 hours between workouts for the same bodypart and you're alternating the workouts. (See Appendix 1 for different options for arranging your split.)

In addition to splitting your workouts into different bodyparts, you'll also start incorporating advanced training techniques into your program. These intensity-boosting techniques allow

you to stress the muscles to a greater degree in various ways that promote growth. Examples include supersets, drop sets, forced reps, cheat reps and pre-exhaust. By including just a few advanced training techniques you can keep your routine fresh and stimulate your muscles with enough variety to help prevent a plateau. Bodybuilders tend to be extreme in thinking more will be better, but it's really not in your best interest to use intensity boosters on every set of every exercise. One or two techniques used on different exercises in each workout is enough to promote muscle building. Too many advanced techniques in your program will only increase your risk of overtraining, which will result in smaller muscles, not bigger.

For the most part you will go back to doing 8 to 12 reps, because this is

The four-day training split can be adjusted to meet your needs. Just be sure to have at least a 48-hour gap between same bodypart workouts.

the rep range that tends to produce the most muscle growth. You will periodically do higher weight/lower reps to build your strength, and you will sometimes do lower weight/higher reps to build your cell mitochondria. On certain exercises it's always a good idea to go with a higher rep range for safety.

WEEKS 1 AND 2
MONDAY AND THURSDAY

EXERCISE	SETS	REPS
Flat-Bench Press *superset with*	5	6-8
Chin-Up*	5	6-8
Incline Dumbbell Press *superset with*	3	8-12
Seated Cable Row	3	8-12
EZ-Bar Curl	5	6-12^
Concentration Curl	3	8-12
Rope Crunch	3	15-20
Captain's Chair *or* Hanging Leg Raise	3	15-20
External Rotation	2	15-20
Internal Rotation	2	15-20

*For each set, do as many reps/sets as you can without assistance, and use assistance for the remainder. If you can complete all sets without assistance, strap on a weight belt.
^Down the rack – start with a warm-up set, move to a weight that allows 6 reps, then move down the rack in three steps, getting in as many reps as you can with each decrease in weight.

Photos by Paul Buceta / Michael Butler
Model Joel Stubbs / David Hughes

WEEKS 1 AND 2
TUESDAY AND FRIDAY

EXERCISE	SETS	REPS
Squat	5	6–8*
Dumbbell Press *or* Barbell Lunge	3	8–12
Leg Extension *superset with* Lying Leg Curl	3 3	15–20 8–12
Stiff-Legged Deadlift	3	8–12
Standing Calf Raise	3	15–20
Seated Calf Raise	3	15–20
Shoulder Press	3	8–12
Dumbbell Lateral Raise	3	8–12
Triceps Dip	3	8–12
Lying Triceps Extension	3	8–12
Crunch	3	15–20
Reverse Crunch	3	15–20

*Make sure to warm up with at least 2 light sets before attempting working sets.

WEEKS 3 AND 4
MONDAY AND THURSDAY

EXERCISE	SETS	REPS
Push-Up on Handles*	5	8–12
Incline Dumbbell Flye	3	8–12
Barbell Row	5	8–12
One-Arm Row	3	8–12
Alternating Curl	5	6–12^
Preacher Curl	3	8–12
Hammer Curl	3	8–12
Hanging Leg Raise *or* Captain's Chair	3	15–20
Knee-In	3	15–20
External Rotation	2	15–20
Internal Rotation	2	15–20

*If these are too easy, lift your feet up on a bench or have someone hold a plate steady on your back.
^Down the rack – start with a warm-up, move to a weight that allows 6 reps, then move down the rack in three
 steps, getting in as many reps as you can with each decrease in weight.

Photo by Paul Buceta
Model Jay Cutler

WEEKS 3 AND 4
TUESDAY AND FRIDAY

EXERCISE	SETS	REPS
Deadlift	5	6-8*
Stiff-Legged Deadlift	3	8-12
Hack Squat	3	8-12
Calf Raise on Hack Squat Machine	3	15-20
Seated Calf Raise	3	15-20
Shoulder Press	3	8-12
Cable Lateral Raise	3	15-20
Bent-Over Cable Lateral Raise	3	15-20
Close-Grip Bench Press	3	8-12
Reverse Cable Extension	3	15-20
Crunch	3	15-20
Reverse Crunch	3	15-20

*Make sure to warm up with at least 2 light sets before attempting working sets.
Note: Take days 3 (Wednesday), 6 (Saturday) and 7 (Sunday) off

SUPPLEMENTS
Protein

The first protein powders manufactured specifically for athletes were introduced to the market in the 1950s. Over the next two decades protein supplements became more popular among bodybuilders and tins of the powder were often given away as prizes at bodybuilding contests. Protein supplements have become one of the most popular ergogenic aids used by bodybuilders, and there is an increasingly wide array of products and brands to choose from. Some of the most popular types of protein powder include whey, casein, egg and soy, along with rice and hemp, each with its own specific purposes.

Protein supplements quickly became a staple in the diets of most bodybuilders following their debut in the 1950s.

Whey

Whey accounts for about 20 percent of the protein in cow's milk, and casein accounts for the other 80 percent. Whey is the most commonly consumed type of protein supplement, largely because of its digestibility, bioavailability (amount absorbed versus amount utilized by the body) and high concentrations of branched-chain amino acids and glutamine. Whey protein also has a very rapid rate of absorption, so it's a beneficial option when you need to quickly get amino acids into your bloodstream to fuel muscle building. Because it can be absorbed faster than any other protein form, whey is the best choice for first thing in the morning as well as pre- and post-workout. From a practical point of view, whey is relatively inexpensive and it mixes into shakes more easily than other types.

Casein

Casein is recognized as a bedtime protein powder because of the slow rate at which it gets released and absorbed in the body. Casein moves through your digestive tract at a gradual pace, providing a steady flow of amino acids into your blood. The amino acids will stay in the bloodstream for a relatively long period, therefore helping fend off catabolism (muscle wasting). In addition, of all the protein powder forms, casein has the highest amount of glutamine, which is a key amino acid that preserves muscle mass. This form of protein can also be used when you know you'll be going more than two or three hours without a meal.

Egg

Egg protein has a moderate absorption rate – it gets absorbed by your body more quickly than casein but more slowly than whey. The main

Photo by Rich Baker

benefits of egg protein are its high biological value (a large percentage of the amino acids get utilized by the body); excellent amino acid profile; and its low-calorie, low-carbohydrate and low-fat nutritional breakdown. Egg protein can be consumed at any meal throughout the day, but it may not be your best option immediately post-workout when you want to get amino acids into your bloodstream as quickly as possible. In addition, despite better refinement procedures, most egg protein supplements need to be mixed in a blender.

Soy

Although sometimes maligned because it contains phytoestrogens, soy is comparable to the other protein types, according to research. Soy is derived from plants, but it's one of the few plant sources that contain the full spectrum of essential amino acids. Most plant sources are deficient in one or more amino acids and are thus called incomplete proteins. Soy, however, is called a complete protein because it has all nine essential aminos. This protein type is also very low in fat, cholesterol and lactose. Soy's phytoestrogens (isoflavones) have been shown in studies to be tissue specific and therefore don't cause estrogenic effects such as bodyfat increase.

Brown Rice

Brown rice protein is a good example of the advancements that have been made in the health-food industry. While regular cooked brown rice has a protein content of only five to seven percent, the process of concentrating it (which involves grinding the rice into flour, then mixing it with water and enzymes) creates an end product that is 80 to 90 percent pure protein. Concentrating

brown rice also changes its amino acid profile. In whole form, the grain doesn't contain adequate amounts of lysine, one of the nine essential amino acids, thus making it an incomplete protein. When concentrated in powdered form, however, brown rice is an excellent complete protein source containing the full spectrum of essential and nonessential amino acids.

> "Protein supplements have become one of the most popular ergogenic aids used by bodybuilders, and there is an increasingly wide array of products and brands to choose from."

Rice protein also contains about five times more arginine than whey protein does. Arginine, another essential amino acid, has been shown to elevate growth hormone levels, boost the immune system and enhance blood flow to the muscles for better energy during workouts and faster recovery afterward.

For individuals who can't tolerate gluten (e.g. those with Celiac disease), brown rice protein is an ideal source because it's gluten free. This type of protein powder is also a good alternative for bodybuilders who are lactose intolerant, as it contains no milk ingredients. In addition, rice protein is a quality source of B vitamins and vitamin E. In comparison to whey and egg protein supplements, which can sometimes cause gastrointestinal upset, users note very little cramping and bloating when taking rice protein.

Hemp

Hemp has become one of nature's most versatile plants, with products ranging from clothing to fuels and plastics to medicines being manufactured from it. Hemp has also become recognized as one of the best plant protein sources available, right alongside soy. Although a plant species, hemp is categorized as a complete protein source because it contains adequate amounts of the essential amino acids necessary to meet an individual's dietary needs. Hemp also provides a three-to-one ratio of omega 6 to omega 3 essential fatty acids needed for a wide variety of physiological and metabolic functions in the body.

"Arginine, another essential amino acid, has been shown to elevate growth hormone levels, boost the immune system and enhance blood flow to the muscles for better energy during workouts."

This plant protein is high in insoluble fiber, which is essential for stabilizing blood sugar levels, promoting digestive health and maintaining bowel regularity. Hemp is also virtually free of artificial sweeteners and preservatives. Some users report that the protein products have an earthy or plant-like taste, but this can be resolved by blending it with fruit or natural-flavored yogurt. Another benefit of hemp protein is that it doesn't seem to cause the gas, cramping and feeling of fullness that some milk- and egg-based protein powders cause.

The one main downside of hemp protein is the cost. It's more expensive than other protein supplements because of the extra care and necessary processes employed to maintain the nutritional content. This is especially true for the essential fatty acids that need refinement to ensure the correct quantity and ratio are present in the end protein product.

Because of the oxidizing properties of plants, hemp degenerates more quickly than milk- and egg-based protein supplements. As a result, hemp is sold only in 1- and 2-pound containers.

How Much

Individual protein needs will vary slightly depending on the individual's body type, level of activity, metabolism and physique goals. While some experts in the fields of nutrition, health and sports don't agree on how much protein an individual needs, the general recommendation for bodybuilders is to aim to get 1.0 to 1.5 grams of protein per pound of bodyweight each day. The majority of your protein should come from whole-food sources such as poultry, fish, beef, pork and eggs. You can make small adjustments to your total daily intake, depending on how your body responds. You should also take into account the phase of training you're in when determining your nutrition plan. You may require slightly different protein:carb:fat ratios for bulking, leaning-out and strength-building periods.

Protein Shakes

When taking protein supplements, always follow label directions for appropriate serving sizes and mixing instructions. Most protein powders can be mixed in a shaker cup, but you can also use a blender if you want to add more ingredients such as fruit, any type of natural nut butter or yogurt.

When deciding how many grams of protein to consume on a daily basis, body-builders generally multiply their weight by 1.0 to 1.5 grams.

Photo by Michael Butler
Model Mark Dugdale

Here's a sample daily meal plan for month four:

Breakfast
- Scrambled eggs prepared with 3 whole eggs, 1 tsp. olive oil, 1 tsp. water, 1 tbsp. low-fat/nonfat milk, ½ cup cooked ham (chopped), ½ cup onion (chopped), salt and pepper
- 1 cup cream of wheat, cooked
- ½ cup low-fat cottage cheese

Mid-Morning Snack
- Protein shake made with 1 to 2 scoops whey protein powder, water (or low-fat/nonfat milk)
- 1 medium-sized apple

Lunch
- Chicken sandwich prepared with 6 to 8 ounces cooked chicken breast (sliced), 2 slices whole-grain bread, 1 oz. cheddar cheese, 1 cup lettuce (shredded), and ½ tomato (sliced)
- 1 cup low-fat plain yogurt
- ¼ cup pumpkin seeds

Mid-Afternoon Snack
- Low-fat bran muffin
- Protein shake made with 1 or 2 scoops whey protein powder, water (or low-fat/nonfat milk)

Dinner
- 8 ounces trout or halibut, grilled
- 1 cup cooked quinoa
- 2 cups mixed greens salad with 1 tbsp. vinaigrette dressing

Before-Bed Snack
- Protein shake prepared with 1 scoop (approximately 25 grams of protein) casein protein powder, water (or low-fat/nonfat milk)

Photo by Paul Buceta
Model Antoine Vaillant

Photo by Kevin Horton
Model Ed van Amsterdam

Photo by Gregory James
Model Manuel Romero

Photo by Gregory James
Model Fred Smalls

STIMULATE GROWTH THROUGH VARIETY

7

CH. 7

STIMULATE GROWTH THROUGH VARIETY

During the fifth month of this program you'll continue with the four-day training split, but we will switch the exercises around to add some variety, keeping you interested and keeping your muscles growing. When you are a beginning bodybuilder, your muscles react to whatever you do, but once they've adapted to the routine your muscles will not continue to grow. This month you will continue with the same split as last month: two workouts twice per week (Monday/Thursday and Tuesday/Friday), and Wednesday, Saturday and Sunday will be rest days. Over the course of the month, you'll incorporate some intensity-boosting techniques in various exercises. Adding advanced training techniques such as giant sets, supersets, drop sets and pyramid sets will challenge your muscles in different ways, stimulating more muscle fibers and encouraging new growth. These types of strategies will keep your muscles "guessing" and help you avoid hitting a training plateau. While you may be tempted to do so, it's best not to use advanced techniques on every set. Research has demonstrated that such a high level of intensity may overtax your body and send you into an overtrained state, especially at this point in your training. For best results, intensity boosters should be used on no more than one or two sets of a few exercises in each workout.

During this month we will also begin playing with numbers of sets and reps. Please keep in mind that the number of reps per set determines how heavy the weight is. Regardless of the number of reps, the last couple in each set should be challenging. So if the reps drop to 5 or 6, that means the weight goes up. If the reps increase to 15 to 20, that means the weight goes down. Bodybuilders often hate dropping the weight, but it's in your best interest to leave your ego at the gym door. Numbers don't make big muscles; proper work does. Occasional higher-rep workouts help enlarge the mitochondria in muscle cells, equaling larger muscles in the long run.

There are several advanced training techniques that you can use to keep your muscles guessing and stimulate them into greater growth.

 (margin, rotated)
Photo by Michael Butler
Model Blair Mone

WEEKS 1 AND 3
MONDAY AND THURSDAY

EXERCISE	SETS	REPS
Incline Bench Press *superset with*	3	8-12
Barbell Row	3	8-12
Cable Crossover *superset with*	3	8-12
Front Lat Pulldown	3	8-12
EZ-Bar Curl	5	8-12*
Preacher Curl	3	12-15
Rope Crunch	3	15-20
Captain's Chair *or* Hanging Leg Raise	3	15-20
External Rotation	2	15-20
Internal Rotation	2	15-20
*Negatives on last set		

Photo by Gregory James
Model Brandon Curry

WEEKS 1 AND 3
TUESDAY AND FRIDAY

EXERCISE	SETS	REPS
Leg Press	3	8-12
Deadlift (from floor)	3	8-12
Lying Leg Curl	3	8-12
Toe Press (on Leg Press Machine)	3	15-20
Seated Calf Raise	3	15-20
Front Barbell Press	3	8-12
Wide-Grip Upright Row	3	8-12
Barbell Shrug	3	8-12
Lying Extension	5	5-12*
Bench Dip	3	15-20
Plank	3	30 seconds (week 1) 50 seconds (week 3)

*Do one or two light warm-up sets, two working sets and then drop sets

WEEKS 2 AND 4
MONDAY AND THURSDAY

EXERCISE	SETS	REPS
Incline Bench Press *giant set with*	2	8-12
Incline Bench Flye	2	8-12
Decline Dumbbell Press	2	8-12
Push-Up	2	15-20
Barbell Row	3	8-12
One-Arm Row	3	8-12
Dumbbell Curl	3	8-12*
Concentration Curl	3	12-15
Rope Crunch	3	15-20
Captain's Chair *or* Hanging Leg Raise	3	15-20
External Rotation	2	15-20
Internal Rotation	2	15-20

*The last set is down the rack

WEEKS 2 AND 4
TUESDAY AND FRIDAY

EXERCISE	SETS	REPS
Smith-Machine Squat	5	8–12*
Lying Leg Curl	3	8–12
Standing Calf Raise	3	15–20
Arnold Press	3	8–12
Cable Lateral Raise *superset with*	3	8–12
Bent-Over Cable Lateral Raise	3	8–12
Barbell Shrug	3	8–12
Dip	3	8–12
Cable Reverse Extension (facing away from pulley)	3	8–12
Plank	3	40 seconds (week 2) 60 seconds (week 4)

*Pyramid set — at your top weight do 5 reps

SUPPLEMENTS
Amino Acids

Amino acids serve as the building blocks of proteins and have many metabolic functions in the body. They're already in digested form, so amino acids get absorbed directly into the bloodstream. As a result, the kidneys and liver are under less stress, because they don't have to help break down and excrete waste byproducts of protein metabolism. Therefore, it would seem to make sense to consume amino acids instead of protein supplements, but there is both scientific and anecdotal evidence suggesting that consuming large quantities of certain amino acids may be harmful – when taken on their own or when combined with other amino acids or supplements. Scientists have not been able to determine the appropriate

> "Some researchers are convinced that when certain amino acids are taken in dosages of two grams or more, a drug-like effect is achieved."

proportions the amino acids should be consumed in when taken in supplemental form. In addition, since there are 22 amino acids (actually scientists argue anywhere from 20 to 28 amino acids exist), individuals would have to buy and consume this many different supplements. Furthermore, amino acids supplements are relatively expensive, as they need to undergo such extensive processing.

One valid argument against amino acid supplements is that they are un-

necessary if you are already getting enough high-quality protein in your diet from whole-food sources. There is also a tendency among some members of society to use medications or supplements as a fast solution to almost every health issue. This growing reliance on pills has the potential to be very dangerous because some individuals will take a substance assuming they need to when they really do not. Ingesting too many amino acid supplements, for example, could be extremely harmful to your health. The human body evolved to remove the amino acids it needs from food in a slow and controlled manner, a digestive process that can be called selective absorption. The body breaks down food at its own pace and removes what it requires on an as-needed basis. Attempting to bypass much of the digestive process by taking a supplement may actually overload your system and disrupt the balance of crucial metabolic reactions.

Despite the potential cons of taking amino acid supplements, some argue that there is enough research to prove bodybuilders can use these products without risking health or injury. Some experts even go as far as suggesting that amino acid supplements are an absolute must to maximize strength and size gains. Since muscle growth is heavily dependent on a positive nitrogen balance, they argue nitrogen-based compounds such as amino acids will have a beneficial impact. The body's nitrogen balance is used by biochemists to measure, among other things, the potential for muscle growth. Positive nitrogen balance indicates that the amount of nitrogen being taken in from protein and amino acids is greater than the amount of nitrogen being excreted. This is the necessary state for amino acids and protein to be convert-

ed into new muscle tissue. Conversely, a negative balance indicates that more nitrogen is being excreted from the body than is being absorbed. When this is the case, the body will have difficulty building new muscle tissue – it may even start burning existing tissue as a fuel source. And when hard-earned muscle is at stake, some bodybuilders will opt for amino acid supplements despite the known risks and extra costs.

Amino Acids as Drugs?

Some researchers are convinced that when certain amino acids are taken in dosages of two grams or more, a drug-like effect is achieved. If symptoms similar to those caused by drugs really do occur, then shouldn't these amino acids be classified as such and be regulated under drug laws (i.e., prescription only)? Unfortunately, the answer is not clearly defined as there's an equally valid counter argument: some health experts believe amino acids, as natural food substances, should remain in the food supplement category.

Taking high dosages of individual amino acids seemed to peak in the 1980s and has declined over the past two decades or so. Most bodybuilders simply can't justify the cost when the results are not major.

Here's a list of some of the amino acids and their documented effects.

AMINO ACID	EFFECT
Serine	Produces energy
Alanine	Improves glycogen storage
Arginine	Promotes growth hormone release
Proline	Repairs tissues
Leucine	Encourages tissue repair and growth; plays a vital role in protein synthesis
Taurine	Counters the effects of aging
Glutamine	Increase nitrogen retention; boosts the immune system
Histidine	Aids protein synthesis
Tryptophan	Induces sleep

Branched Chain Amino Acids – BCAAs

This group of three amino acids (leucine, isoleucine and valine) is aptly named branched chain amino acids because of its molecular structure with side chains that branch off. BCAAs are among the eight essential amino acids and they get absorbed rapidly in the body. For bodybuilders and other strength athletes, BCAAs are especially important because they get metabolized in the muscle rather than the liver. That means they're almost immediately available in muscle tissue to build new proteins or get burned as fuel to produce energy. It's also been theorized that after muscle cells take in BCAAs, the body will increase the absorption of other amino acids to keep everything in balance. Research has demonstrated that BCAAs can also reduce fatigue in both anaerobic and endurance training. In addition, studies have determined that leucine has powerful anti-catabolic properties and plays a vital role in protein synthesis.

The suggested dosage for BCAAs is 1 to 4 grams taken 60 to 90 minutes after your workout.

Branched chain amino acids are metabolized in the muscle and are therefore very rapidly available to the body to use for energy.

Photo by Rich Baker

Working out is essential, but you must also follow a well-balanced daily meal plan in order to build an awe-inspiring body.

Here's a sample daily meal plan for month five:

Breakfast
- Apple flax pancakes prepared with 1 egg, 1 tbsp. plain yogurt, 1 packet (equal to 1 gram) artificial sweetener, ¼ tsp. vanilla, 2 tbsp. flax meal (ground flax seeds), ½ an apple (chopped into small pieces), pinch of cinnamon, olive oil cooking spray (to coat griddle or skillet)
- 1 cup 100% fruit juice

Mid-Morning Snack
- Protein shake made with 1 to 2 scoops whey protein powder, water (or low-fat/nonfat milk)
- 1 cup mixed fresh berries (raspberries, blackberries, blueberries, strawberries)

Lunch
- Chicken pita prepared with 6 to 8 ounces grilled chicken breast, 1 cup chopped romaine lettuce,

¼ cup sliced cucumber, dressing (made with ½ cup low-fat plain yogurt, 1 tbsp. dry mustard, 1 minced garlic clove, 1 tbsp. anchovy paste)

Mid-Afternoon Snack
- Protein shake made with 1 or 2 scoops whey protein powder, water (or low-fat/nonfat milk)
- 1 slice whole-grain toast with 1–2 tbsp. natural nut butter (e.g., peanut or almond)

Dinner
- Pasta prepared with 6 to 8 ounces extra-lean ground beef (browned in skillet and extra fat drained), 1 cup tomato sauce, 1 cup cooked whole-wheat pasta
- 1 cup steamed vegetables
- ½ cup cottage cheese

Before-Bed Snack
- Protein shake prepared with 1 scoop (approximately 25 grams of protein) casein protein powder, water (or low-fat/nonfat milk)

Photo by Gregory James
Model Chris White

Photo by Paul Buceta
Model Evgeni Mishin

Photo by Paul Buceta
Model Tricky Jackson

Photo by Michael Butler
Model Ryan Foxx

Photo by Jason Breeze
Model Gustavo Badell

HALFTIME

CH. 8

HALFTIME

During the sixth month on this program you'll continue to train four days a week, performing a workout for chest, shoulders, triceps, rotator cuffs and abs on Mondays and Thursdays, and a session for legs, back and biceps on Tuesdays and Fridays. You will continue to add intensity techniques to different exercises and use them more often.

At this point you will have to pay attention to paying attention. You are no longer a new bodybuilder, and this is the stage where you might start to get a little lazy – letting your mind wander during workouts, not putting forth as much effort as you should or going through the motions. If you find yourself going into that zone, then stop! When you're in the gym you're there for a purpose, and that purpose is to build muscle. Pick up girls later. Worry about work later. Generally speaking, whatever you have going on in your life can wait. Use your gym time efficiently. Pay attention to doing all the little things right and never take shortcuts. Make sure to do a light warm-up set before starting the working sets for each bodypart.

Don't allow boredom to ruin your plan. Keep your eye on the prize and make the most out of every workout.

Photos by Gregory James / Rich Baker
Models Lee Banks / Eduardo Corrêa da Silva

WEEKS 1 AND 2
MONDAY AND THURSDAY

EXERCISE	SETS	REPS
Incline Dumbbell Press	5	6–8
Flat-Bench Dumbbell Flye	3	8–12
Barbell Upright Row *triset with*	3	12–15
Dumbbell Lateral Raise	3	12–15
Bent-Over Lateral Raise	3	12–15
Skullcrusher	3	8–12
Dip (add weight belt if necessary)	3	8–12
One-Arm Cable Extension	3	8–12
External Rotation	2	15–20
Internal Rotation	2	15–20
Swiss Ball Crunch	2	25
Reverse Crunch	3	15–20

Photo by Jason Breeze
Model Darrem Charles

WEEKS 1 AND 2
TUESDAY AND FRIDAY

EXERCISE	SETS	REPS
Squat	5	6–8
Hack Squat	3	8–12
Stiff-Legged Deadlift	3	8–12
Standing Calf Raise	3	15–20
Seated Calf Raise	3	15–20
Chin-Up	3	10*
T-Bar Row	3	8–12
Hyperextension	2	20
EZ-Bar Curl	3	8–12
Dumbbell Curl	5	6–15^
Wrist Curl	2	20
Reverse Wrist Curl	2	20
Plank	3	1 minute

*If you can't do 3 sets of 10 reps, do as many sets as necessary until you achieve 30 total reps
^Drop sets

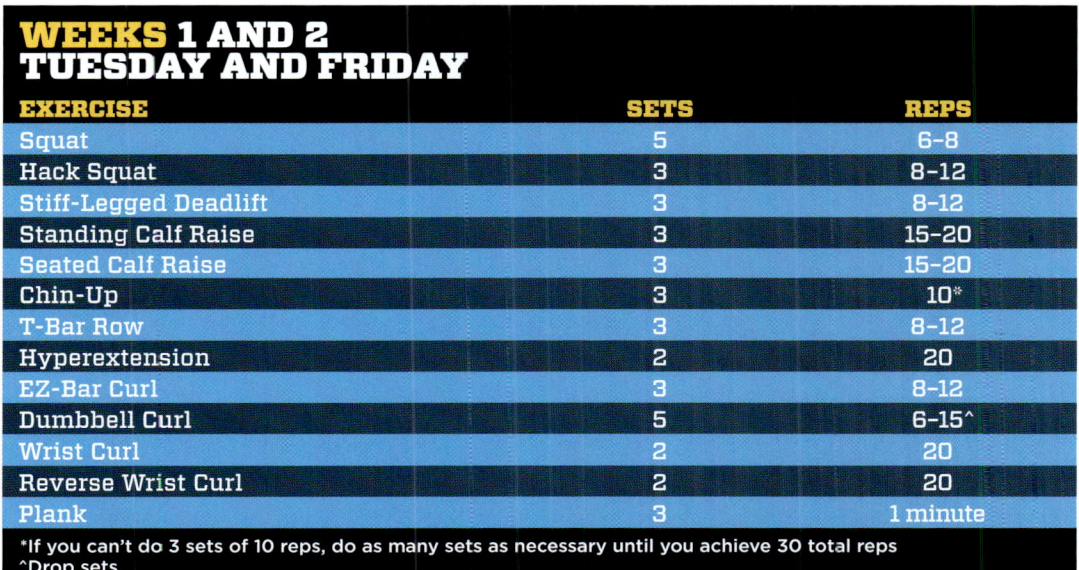

Photo by Paul Buceta
Model Antoine Vaillant

WEEKS 3 AND 4
MONDAY AND THURSDAY

EXERCISE	SETS	REPS
Flat-Bench Press	5	6–8
Cable Crossover	3	12–15
Close-Grip Bench Press	3	8–12
Bench Dip (add weight plates)	3	8–12
Triceps Pressdown	5	12–15
Front Press	5	6–8
Cable Lateral Raise	3	12–15
Bent-Over Cable Lateral Raise	3	12–15
Captain's Chair *or* Hanging Leg Raise	3	12–15
Twisting Captain's Chair *or* Hanging Leg Raise	3	12–15
External Rotation	2	15–20
Internal Rotation	2	15–20

Photo by Ralph DeHaan
Model: Branch Warren

Photo by Paul Buceta
Model Hidetada Yamagishi

WEEKS 3 AND 4
TUESDAY AND FRIDAY

EXERCISE	SETS	REPS
Deadlift	5	6-8
Leg Press	3	8-12
Toe Press	3	15-20
Lying Leg Curl	3	8-12
Seated Row	5	6-8
One-Arm Row	3	8-12
Barbell Curl	5	6-15*
Hammer Curl	5	6-15
Preacher Curl	3	12-15
Wrist Roller	5	up and down
Plank	3	1 minute

*Drop sets

SUPPLEMENTS
ZMA

ZMA is a scientifically manufactured mineral formula containing zinc mono-methionine aspartate and magnesium aspartate, along with vitamin B-6. Manufacturers claim ZMA increases anabolic hormone levels and helps improve muscular strength, though some studies report inconsistent results.

ZMA was first developed by Victor Conte, the founder of BALCO Laboratories. Initial research performed by BALCO observed that athletes often had mineral deficiencies, including zinc and magnesium. Both zinc and magnesium are essential minerals; zinc plays a major role in testosterone production and magnesium helps oxygenate muscle tissue. If a bodybuilder or strength athlete were deficient in either, muscle-building potential would theoretically be negatively impacted.

Multivitamin formulations often contain identical amounts of these two minerals, but some experts argue that taking a ZMA product separately is more effective. Their reasoning is based on the theory of competing nutrients. Because calcium is known to block zinc and magnesium absorption and calcium is present in multivitamins, they suggest we do not absorb zinc and magnesium as efficiently when we get them from this source. In addition, the calcium present in multivitamins is more readily absorbed by the stomach, so the zinc and magnesium are purportedly excreted more often when consumed this way.

Studies have demonstrated that ZMA supplementation may have a positive effect on sleep habits. This benefit is especially important to bodybuilders because adequate rest and proper sleep are crucial to recovery and mus-

Photo by Rich Baker
Model Marco Cardona

Sleep and relaxation give your body the chance to recover from daily activities, and also lead to new muscle tissue growth.

cle growth. It is during the hours of sleep that many anabolic hormones (including testosterone and growth hormone) are released in greater concentrations. During this time, most of the body's new muscle tissue is built and repaired.

Most ZMA products contain 30 milligrams of zinc, 450 milligrams of magnesium and 11 milligrams of vitamin B-6. The general recommendation is to take ZMA before bed on an empty stomach (approximately two hours after your last meal and at least 30 minutes before you take any other bedtime supplements), but always follow the label directions.

Prohormones

Prohormones did not become mainstream substances until 1998 when a reporter spotted the supplement androstenedione, or "Andro," in the locker

of Major League Baseball player Mark McGwire. With the publicity surrounding McGwire's admission to taking the supplement – and the fact he broke Roger Maris' home-run record that season – androstenedione gained renewed popularity and sales greatly increased.

Prohormones are classified as precursors to hormones. They came on the market in large part as a direct

> "It is during the hours of sleep that many anabolic hormones (including testosterone and growth hormone) are released in greater concentrations."

result of the reclassification of anabolic steroids as illegal substances in 1990. Recognizing that many former steroid users would be looking for a legal supplement alternative, manufacturers started hiring biochemists to synthesize a new class of supplements that possessed steroid-like effects but were still considered legal (at the time). The effectiveness and safety of prohormones have been debated since their introduction. In 2004, the Anabolic Control Act was amended to include prohormones as illegal substances.

Here's a brief overview of prohormones and the terms commonly used to describe them. Androstenedione, for example, is a molecule very similar to testosterone. The primary difference between the two is that where testosterone has a hydroxyl group (a hydrogen and oxygen atom bonded together, written as -OH) in a certain position, androstenedione has a keto group (a carbon and oxygen atom joined by a double bond, expressed as C=O). In the

While some bodybuilders use Andro, it's worth noting that it may lead to various side effects including gynecomastia and a higher risk of prostate cancer.

most simplistic terms, androstenedione is a precursor to testosterone.

The body can convert androstenedione to testosterone (and vice versa) by use of a specific enzyme present in reasonably large amounts within the body. Oral supplementation with Andro very briefly increases blood levels of testosterone, and it is this ability to act as a direct hormonal predecessor of testosterone that makes it attractive to bodybuilders and other athletes. However, while androstenedione is a precursor of testosterone, it is also a precursor of estrone, which is an estrogenic hormone. As a result, this prohormone can have adverse estrogenic effects similar to those of anabolic steroids, such as gynecomastia (abnormal development of the mammary glands causing breast enlargement). In addition, androstenedione can convert to a potent androgenic compound known as dihydrotestosterone (DHT). Increased DHT levels can sometimes lead to hair and skin problems, as well as a higher instance of prostate cancer.

Other variations of androstenedione are available, including 4-androstenediol (4-AD) and 5-androstenediol (5-AD), which differ chemically by the position of the chemical double bond in the steroid molecule (explaining the numeric designations in their names). Like androstenedione, these versions create both androgenic and estrogenic activity (in the case of 4-androstendiol, however, the estrogenic conversion is only indirect).

Another group of prohormones called NorAndro products are precursors of a compound called nortestosterone. Also called nandrolone, this sex hormone is found in certain animals, including horses. This prohormone makes up half the content of the anabolic steroid nandrolone decanoate (also known as Deca-

Photo by Gregory James
Model Adam Headland

Nandrolene is a sex hormone found in several animals. This prohormone was banned in 2004 when it was added to the Controlled Substances Act.

Durabolin). In comparison to testosterone, nandrolone exhibits higher anabolic activity in humans in relation to its androgenic activity. Since nandrolone metabolizes to a weaker compound than testosterone does (called dihydronandrolone), precursors of nandrolone are much less likely than testosterone to cause hair, skin and other androgenic problems. Variations include 19-nor-4-androstenedione (19-nordione), 19-nor-4-androstenediol and 19-nor-5-androstenediol (19-nordiols). Here again, the numbers indicate the relative positions of the primary bonds in the molecule. All andro supplements and prohormones were added to the Controlled Substances Act in 2004 and remain banned supplements.

Tribulus Terrestris

Tribulus terrestris (also known as puncture vine) is a flowering plant that grows in temperate and tropical

Tribulus terrestris: this herb is believed to improve sex drive, increase testosterone levels and promote the growth of impressive muscles.

Photo by Gregory James
Model Ahmad Ahmad

climates, and is popular in traditional Chinese medicine. As a dietary supplement, manufacturers claim *Tribulus terrestris* has many metabolic properties and can increase testosterone levels, promote muscle growth and improve sex drive. There are also reports that this herb can treat colic pains, lower blood pressure and reduce cholesterol levels.

Researchers have determined that *Tribulus* likely works by increasing the body's levels of luteinizing hormone (LH), which is produced by the pituitary gland. In turn, LH stimulates the testes to boost production of testosterone. With more testosterone circulating in the body, muscle growth and strength building are augmented – that's one of

the main reasons synthetic testosterone and related testosterone-boosting
supplements are so popular. Keep in
mind, however, that *Tribulus* is not a
hormone supplement. By increasing
the production of testosterone, the
herb works only within the body's natural limits to help users achieve their
strength and muscular potential. *Tribulus* will not cause the body to produce more testosterone on an ongoing
basis; instead, it balances natural hormone levels. *Tribulus terrestris* is most
effective when taken by those who
participate in regular, strenuous training with proper recovery periods. For
best results, anecdotal evidence suggests individuals take 750 to 1,500
milligrams per day.

Here's a sample daily meal plan for
month six:

Breakfast
- Applesauce oatmeal pancakes
  prepared with ¼ cup all-purpose
  flour, ¼ cup whole-wheat flour,
  ½ cup steel-cut oats, 1 tsp. baking
  powder, ½ tsp. baking soda, ¼ tsp.
  salt, ½ cup low-fat (1%) milk,
  ½ cup applesauce, 2 egg whites,
  ¼ cup sugar, 1 tbsp. olive oil
- 1 cup low-fat cottage cheese
- 1 medium-sized peach

Mid-Morning Snack
- Low-fat bran muffin
- Protein shake made with 1 to 2
  scoops whey protein powder,
  water (or low-fat/nonfat milk)

Lunch
- Greek burger prepared with
  8 ounces extra-lean (95%) ground
  beef, ½ cup crumbled feta cheese,
  ½ cup sliced olives, 3 cloves
  chopped garlic, and salt and pep-

per (to taste); whole-grain bun,
tomato, lettuce, onion, mustard

Mid-Afternoon Snack
- Protein shake made with 1 or 2
  scoops whey protein powder,
  water (or low-fat/nonfat milk)
- ¼ cup almonds

Dinner
- 6 ounces grilled halibut
- 1 cup brown rice
- 2 cups spinach salad with
  chopped tomatoes, celery, cucumber, red pepper; low-fat dressing

Before-Bed Snack
- Protein shake prepared with
  1 scoop (approximately 25 grams
  of protein) casein protein powder,
  water (or low-fat/nonfat milk)

Photo by Gregory James
Model Joel Stubbs

Photo by Gregory James
Model Lou Joseph

Photo by Paul Buceta
Model Jojo Ntiforo

Photo by Paul Buceta
Model Ahmad Haidar

ATTENTION TO DETAIL

Photo by Paul Buceta
Model Manuel Romero

ATTENTION TO DETAIL

Adding variety to your routine on a regular basis is always important. Remember that muscles adapt and they can't continue to grow unless they are stressed in different ways. Making modifications to exercise order, set-and-rep schemes and hand grips, as well as changing up the exercises you perform for each bodypart, will help promote continuous growth and decrease your chances of hitting a rut with your training.

When you were a new bodybuilder you had to really concentrate on doing the exercises correctly, holding your body in the right positions and figuring out which weight to use for the chosen rep schemes. Now you can start think-

Photo by Gregory James / Illustration courtesy ©iStockphoto.com/MMIAD
Model Marcus Haley

If you're getting bored, modify the way you're performing the exercise. Changing hand grips and set-and-rep schemes can make a significant difference.

ing about how each exercise feels for you, and what results you get from it. You'll find that an exercise your buddy swears by does nothing for you. Conversely, you may get the best pump of your life from an exercise others say is useless. You should also start playing with positions during exercises (safely, of course). A slight shift in your grip or foot stance may be exactly what you need to hit a lagging muscle. A different set-and-rep scheme may also help you reap muscular rewards.

Move those weights and be conscious every second of the muscle fibers working, and sometimes breaking, to help you accomplish your goal. If you find yourself getting bored with a particular exercise then go ahead and switch it up with an exercise that works the same muscle in a similar way – Appendix 2 has lots of options for you.

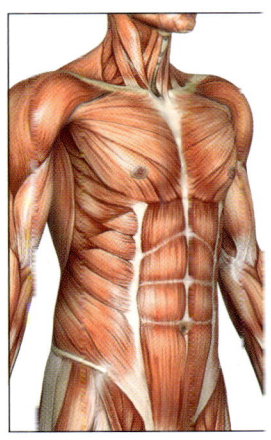

Don't forget you're going to the gym for a reason. To reap the rewards, you'll have to stay focused.

WEEKS 1 AND 2
MONDAY AND THURSDAY

EXERCISE	SETS	REPS
Incline Dumbbell Press *superset with*	3	8–12
Dumbbell Flye	3	8–12
Pull-Up (from hanging)	2	20^
Seated Cable Row	3	8–12
Weighted Dip	3	8–12
One-Arm Reverse Pressdown	4	12–15
EZ-Bar Curl	4	8–12*
Concentration Curl	5	8–12
Upright Row	3	8–12
Dumbbell Lateral Raise	3	15–20
Bent-Over Cable Row	3	15–20
Wrist Roller	5	up and down

^Use rest-pause to get up to a total of 20 reps per set
*Do negatives on the last set

Photo by Michael Butler
Model Silvio Samuel

WEEKS 1 AND 2
TUESDAY AND FRIDAY

EXERCISE	SETS	REPS
Barbell Squat	5	5–12*
Leg Extension	3	8–12
Lying Leg Curl	3	8–12
Standing Calf Raise	3	15–20
Seated Calf Raise	3	15–20
Rope Crunch	3	15–20
Knee-In	3	15–20
Plank	3	60 seconds
External Rotation	2	15–20
Internal Rotation	2	15–20

*Make sure to warm up adequately, do a working set or two and then drop weight each set.

WEEKS 3 AND 4
MONDAY AND THURSDAY

EXERCISE	SETS	REPS
Bench Press	5	5–12*
Cable Crossover (from floor)	3	8–12
Barbell Shrug	3	8–12
Front Barbell Press	3	8–12
Lying Extension	5	5–12*
Triceps Pressdown	3	15–20
Barbell Row	3	6–8
One-Arm Row	3	8–12
Alternating Dumbbell Curl	5	6–8
Arnold Concentration Curl	3	15–20
Wrist Curl (on bench)	2	15–20
Reverse Wrist Curl (on bench)	2	15–20

*Make sure to warm up adequately, do a working set or two and then drop weight each set.

Photos by Gregory James / Paul Buceta
Models Toney Freeman / Quincy Taylor

WEEKS 3 AND 4
TUESDAY AND FRIDAY

EXERCISE	SETS	REPS
Deadlift	2	8-12
Leg Press	5	5-12*
Toe Press	3	15-20
Seated Calf Raise	3	15-20
Captain's Chair *or* Hanging Leg Raise	3	12-15
Twisting Captain's Chair *or* Twisting Hanging Leg Raise	3	12-15
Ab Wheel Rollout	1	8-12
External Rotation	2	15-20
Internal Rotation	2	15-20

*Do a warm-up set first, then pyramid

SUPPLEMENTS

Beta-Alanine

Beta-alanine is a non-essential amino acid, and it is the only amino that occurs naturally in the body. It is also known as 3-aminopropanoic acid and is classified as a non-proteinogenic amino acid, meaning it cannot be synthesized into a protein. Certain research studies suggest beta-alanine supplementation can increase performance because beta-alanine is a precursor for carnosine in muscles. Carnosine is a naturally occurring dipeptide found in both slow- and fast-twitch muscle fibers (Type I and Type II, respectively), but its concentration is significantly higher in fast-twitch fibers. These Type II fibers fire rapidly and are efficient at generating short bursts of strength or speed – it's this type that are primarily used in high-intensity strength workouts and are most responsive to muscular growth. Carnosine works by neutralizing the acidic environment created by metabolizing muscle cells. When cellular environments become too acidic, the muscle stops contracting. Acting as an acidic buffer, carnosine allows bodybuilders to train harder, increase fat burning and thus burn more calories. The best dietary sources are those containing the carnosine (or anserine or balenine) dipeptides. These dipeptides are found in protein-rich foods such as beef, pork, chicken and fish. In supplemental form, the suggested dosage is 3 to 6 grams per day to boost muscle carnosine levels.

Yohimbine

Yohimbine is an alkaloid that is extracted from the inner bark of the *Pausinystalia yohimbe*, a tree that is native to Africa. For centuries *yohimbe* was used in traditional medicine as an aphrodisiac. Recent research has demonstrated that yohimbine is an active ingredient with potent fat-mobilizing capabilities. In the body, active alpha-receptors limit the amount of fat that can be released from storage. Yohimbine works by inhibiting these alpha-receptors on fat cells. When the receptors get shut down with the presence of yohimbine, more fat gets released into the bloodstream to be burned as an energy source.

The recommended dosage is 2–20 milligrams of yohimbine, taken three times daily, ideally in the morning, and then between meals in the afternoon.

On training days, take one dose 30 minutes before working out. Yohimbine should be ingested on an empty stomach, as taking it with a meal may reduce its fat-burning effects. **Editor's note:** Yohimbine is currently not an approved substance in Canada.

CLA

CLA (conjugated linoleic acid) is a polyunsaturated fat derived from lineoleic acid. It often gets overlooked as a fat-loss supplement, despite the fact it has over two decades of research backing its efficacy. Studies have noted that CLA seems to work via three pathways. One is by interfering with lipoprotein lipase – an enzyme that increases fat storage in the body. CLA appears to exert this effect directly on adipocytes (the principle sites of fat storage) and in skeletal muscle cells (the primary

Not only does caffeine provide countless Americans with a morning boost, it also has the ability to maximize fat burning.

sites of fat combustion). Another mechanism of action by which CLA works involves making existing fat deposits more available for use as an energy source. Finally, because CLA promotes lean muscle gain, it increases metabolism and thus positively effects fat burning. For fat reduction, the recommended dosage is 3–5 milligrams three times daily with meals.

Caffeine

Caffeine is a well-documented central-nervous-system (CNS) stimulant that provides a temporary boost shortly after it's consumed. Caffeine is also effective because it elevates metabolism and encourages fat mobilization from storage in fat cells. It's these two effects combined that make caffeine such an excellent fat burner because they interact synergistically to maximize thermogenesis (fat burning). To optimize fat burning, bodybuilders should take 100 to 200 milligrams every four or five hours. About one hour before your workout, this amount can be increased to 200 to 400 milligrams. Individual tolerance to caffeine will vary, so start with the lowest dose and work your way up, depending on how your body handles the caffeine. Anhydrous caffeine has been shown in studies to be the most effective supplemental form of caffeine, but caffeinated coffee can be substituted for one or two doses per day.

Nitric Oxide

Nitric oxide (NO) is a molecule made up of one nitrogen atom and one oxygen atom. A free-form gas produced by the body, nitric oxide is used to communicate with other bodily cells. Nitric-oxide production occurs in the body when enzymes in the body break down arginine. More specifically, NO is

Photo by Robert Reiff
Model Hidetada Yamagishi

generated inside the endothelial cells that line the inside of blood vessels. When endothelial cells are stimulated – for example, during muscle contraction – NO is synthesized and released. From there it diffuses across the cell membrane into the adjacent smooth muscle tissue of the blood vessels, causing them to relax and widen (a process called vasodilation).

For bodybuilders, nitric oxide is important primarily because it increases blood flow. When circulation is improved, more nutrients get transported to the muscle cells, therefore promoting muscle growth. Research has demonstrated that NO also boosts recovery and reduces joint and muscle pain. These anti-inflammatory properties of nitric acid are very beneficial to bodybuilders and other athletes, since regular, intense training taxes the joints and muscles to a great degree.

Most nitric-oxide supplements on the market do not contain the actual NO molecule; instead, they contain the precursor, arginine. The most common side effects are diarrhea, nausea and weakness when taking more than 5 to 10 grams per day. Many protein powders are fortified with amino acids, including arginine, so just be aware of how much total arginine you are taking in from all of your supplements.

Here is a sample daily meal plan for month seven:

Breakfast
- French toast prepared with 2 slices whole-grain bread, 1 tbsp. low-fat (1%) milk, 1 egg white, ¼ tsp. vanilla, ¼ tsp. cinnamon, cooking spray (to coat griddle/skillet)
- ½ cup low-fat Greek yogurt
- 1 cup mixed berries (blueberries, raspberries, blackberries, strawberries)

Mid-Morning Snack
- 1 medium-sized banana
- Protein shake made with 1 to 2 scoops whey protein powder, water (or low-fat/nonfat milk)

Lunch
- 6 ounces broiled or baked chicken breast
- 1 cup salad prepared with mixed greens, chopped tomatoes, chopped red onion, 2 tbsp. crumbled feta cheese, 1 tbsp. low-fat balsamic dressing

"Individual tolerance to caffeine will vary, so start with the lowest dose and work your way up, depending on how your body handles the caffeine."

Mid-Afternoon Snack
- Whole-wheat turkey wrap made with 1 soft whole-wheat tortilla, 5 ounces sliced turkey breast, lettuce, mustard, pepper (to taste)

Dinner
- 6 to 8 ounces grilled flank steak prepared with 1 tbsp. olive oil, 2 tbsp. vinegar, ½ tsp. basil, ½ tsp. parsley (marinate for at least two hours or up to 24 hours)
- 1 cup grilled vegetables (e.g., zucchini, eggplant, peppers)
- 1 (4 ounces) baked sweet potato

Before-Bed Snack
- Protein shake prepared with 1 scoop (approximately 25 grams of protein) casein protein powder, water (or low-fat/nonfat milk)

Photo by Paul Buceta
Model Steve Kuclo

Photo by Kevin Horton
Model Mike Brown

Photo by Paul Buceta
Model Leo Ingram

Photo by Paul Buceta
Model Morris Mendez

CRAZY EIGHT

10

CH. 10

Photo by Paul Buceta
Model Mark Dugdale

CRAZY EIGHT

By this stage in the program, you have likely made noticeable size and strength improvements. As you get stronger, you should be making gradual increases to your working weights on most exercises. When selecting your weight for each movement, it's important to choose appropriate poundage that allows you to reach the target rep range listed. If you can complete more than the upper number in the rep range for a particular exercise, the weight is too light. Conversely, if you have trouble reaching the lower number in the range, the weight is too heavy. The key point to remember is that you still need to challenge your muscles enough to stimulate growth, and that task becomes more difficult as your muscles continue to adapt to the work you give them.

To challenge your muscles in different ways, it's great, on occasion, to do workouts that are extra heavy or extra light (the latter of which can be tough for bodybuilders, but I highly recommend it once in a while). While the 8-to-12 rep range is proven best for stimulating muscle growth, using heavier weights periodically will increase your strength, thereby enabling you to use heavier weights for your regular workouts. Periodically using lighter weights for a high number of reps helps with your muscular endurance, builds the cell mitochondria (which pumps up your muscle) and simply shocks your muscle in a different way. You may be surprised how sore you get after a low-weight/high-rep workout. This month starts with some basic heavy work. Be sure to do a couple of light warm-up sets on every exercise before getting to the heavy poundage. During the third week you'll do a regular 8-to-12-rep routine, and in the fourth week you'll shock your muscles with something they're not expecting: long sets of light weights. At first, you may wonder why you're using lighter weights. But, rest assured, your muscles will eventually thank you because in the long run, you'll experience greater gains.

While decreasing the amount you lift might seem counterproductive, the shock it provides your muscles could be exactly what you need to stimulate growth.

Photo by Paul Buceta
Model Brian Shaw

WEEKS 1 AND 2
MONDAY AND THURSDAY

EXERCISE	SETS	REPS
Flat-Bench Press	3	4–6
Weighted Pull-Up	3	4–6
Barbell Row	3	4–6
Shoulder Press	3	4–6
Weighted Dip	3	4–6
Barbell Curl	3	4–6

Note: Do 1 or 2 warm-up sets before moving on to these work sets.

WEEKS 1 AND 2
TUESDAY AND FRIDAY

EXERCISE	SETS	REPS
Squat	5	4–6
Deadlift	5	4–6
Crunch	3	15–20
Reverse Crunch	3	15–20
External Rotation	2	15–20
Internal Rotation	2	15–20

Note: Do 2 warm-up sets before your work sets.

Photos by Jason Breeze
Models Craig Richardson / Alfonso del Rio

WEEK 3
MONDAY AND THURSDAY

EXERCISE	SETS	REPS
Incline Dumbbell Press	3	8-12
Incline Dumbbell Flye	3	8-12
Seated Cable Row	3	8-12
One-Arm Row	3	8-12
Cable Lateral Raise	3	8-12
Cable Rear Lateral Raise	3	8-12
Lying Extension	3	8-12
Triceps Pressdown	3	8-12
EZ-Bar Curl	3	8-12
Concentration Curl	3	8-12

WEEK 3
TUESDAY AND FRIDAY

EXERCISE	SETS	REPS
Hack Squat	3	8-12
Leg Press	3	8-12
Toe Press	3	15-20
Stiff-Legged Deadlift	3	8-12
Lying Leg Curl	3	8-12
Seated Calf Raise	3	15-20
Captain's Chair *or* Hanging Leg Raise	3	15-20
External Rotation	2	15-20
Internal Rotation	2	15-20

Photos by Gregory James / Paul Buceta
Model Ronny Rockel / Ed Nunn

WEEK 4
MONDAY AND THURSDAY

EXERCISE	SETS	REPS
Flat-Bench Press	3	15-20
Incline Dumbbell Press	3	15-20
Lat Pulldown	3	15-20
T-Bar Row	3	15-20
One-Arm Cable Row (Lawnmower Pull)	3	15-20
Front Barbell Press	3	15-20
Cable Lateral Raise	3	15-20
Lying Extension	3	15-20
One-Arm Reverse Cable Pressdown	3	15-20
Alternating Curl	3	15-20
Preacher Curl	3	15-20

Photo by Kevin Horton
Model Ben Pakulski

WEEK 4
TUESDAY AND FRIDAY

EXERCISE	SETS	REPS
Smith-Machine Squat	3	15–20
Leg Extension	3	15–20
Stiff-Legged Deadlift	3	15–20
Lying Leg Curl	3	15–20
Standing Calf Raise	3	15–20
Seated Calf Raise	3	15–20
Crunch	3	15–20
Knee-In	3	15–20
External Rotation	2	15–20
Internal Rotation	2	15–20

Note: Take days 3 (Wednesday), 6 (Saturday) and 7 (Sunday) off throughout this month.

Photo by Paul Buceta
Model Tricky Jackson

SUPPLEMENTS
Essential Fatty Acids (EFAs)

Certain types of fat are just as vital for various bodily processes as protein and carbohydrates are. Not only are dietary fats necessary for metabolic functions, they're also required for proper absorption, transportation and utilization of the fat-soluble vitamins. In addition, specific forms of fat are used by the body to produce cellular components and hormones. For individuals who are trying to make physique improvements, a moderate intake of the right kinds of fat – with essential fatty acids ranking high on that list – is beneficial to maximize body composition and decrease bodyfat levels.

> "As a fat-loss aid, EFAs – particularly omega-3s – work by increasing fatty acid oxidation and boosting basal metabolic rates."

By consuming the right types of fat, you are actually improving your chances of decreasing bodyfat levels and attaining your dream physique.

Biochemically, essential fatty acids, or EFAs, are long-chain polyunsaturated fatty acids. There are two families of EFAs: omega-3 and omega-6, which are derived from linolenic acids and linoleic acids, respectively. The human body doesn't have the capacity to synthesize these acids, meaning they must be obtained through diet. Omega-9 fatty acids (derived from oleic acids) are part of this group of fatty acids, though they're considered non-essential because the body can produce them on its own if enough omega-3s and omega-6s are present.

EFAs are necessary to support the cardiovascular, reproductive, immune and nervous systems in the body, as well as to manufacture and repair cell membranes. A primary function of EFAs is to produce prostaglandins, hormone-like elements that regulate heart rate, blood pressure and blood clotting, and they play a role in immune function by regulating inflammation and encouraging the body to combat infection. The USDA has not established dietary reference intakes for essential fatty acids, but the "adequate intake" for adult males is approximately 1.6 grams per day.

A deficiency in EFAs may increase an individual's risk of conditions such as hardening of the arteries, abnormal blood clot formation, coronary heart disease, high cholesterol and high blood pressure.

Specifically as a fat-loss aid, EFAs – particularly omega-3s – work by increasing fatty acid oxidation and boosting basal metabolic rates.

Photo by Rich Baker
Model Johnnie Jackson

Here is a sample daily meal plan for month eight:

Breakfast
- Artichoke, spinach and feta omelet prepared with 6 egg whites, ½ tsp. onion powder, 2 cups spinach (or 1 cup thawed frozen), 1 ounce feta cheese, 2 chopped artichoke hearts, cooking spray (to coat skillet)

Mid-Morning Snack
- 2 slices whole-grain toast with 1 tbsp. natural almond butter
- Protein shake made with 1 or 2 scoops whey protein powder, water (or low-fat/nonfat milk)

Lunch
- 6 ounces grilled halibut fillet
- 5 ounces baked potato
- 1 cup mixed greens with low-fat dressing

Mid-Afternoon Snack
- 1 medium-sized apple
- Protein shake made with 1 or 2 scoops whey protein powder, water (or low-fat/nonfat milk)

Dinner
- Coconut chicken prepared with 6 to 8 ounces chicken breast, ½ cup shredded coconut, 2 cups chopped broccoli, 3 chopped garlic cloves, 2 tbsp. olive oil, 2 tbsp. lemon juice, salt and pepper (to taste)

Before-Bed Snack
- Protein shake prepared with 1 scoop (approximately 25 grams of protein) casein protein powder, water (or low-fat/nonfat milk)

Photo by Robert Reiff
Model Tony Breznik

A well-rounded meal plan including a variety of fruits and vegetables is an integral part of your quest to reach your muscular and self-confident best.

Photo by Jason Mathas
Model Jay Cutler

Photo by Paul Buceta
Model Sami Al Haddad

Photo by Ralph DeHaan
Model Omar Deckard

Photo by Gregory James
Model Peter Putnam

PRE-EXHAUST

11

CH. 11

PRE-EXHAUST

During month nine you will go back to the basic muscle-building rep range of 8 to 12, and you will return to doing some intensity techniques. You should find after the last month of performing some lower reps/heavier weights plus the week of higher reps that your strength will have increased. Make use of it – use those heavier weights in the muscle-building range to really get your muscles growing! Your new intensity technique will be "pre-exhaust." The pre-exhaust system was developed by *MuscleMag International* publisher Robert Kennedy, and it has been used by many professional bodybuilders since its creation. Mr. Kennedy realized that often trainees are limited in how much weight they can use on the big compound exercises, not because of weakness of the muscle being worked, but rather by the limitations of the smaller assisting muscles. For example, when doing barbell rows your lats might be able to give you more reps but your biceps, an assisting muscle, will prevent you from doing so. The solution is to pre-exhaust your lats with an isolation exercise first, so by the time your biceps are giving out on rows your lats are also finished.

By now you should be getting a feel for how your body responds and how you should feel on an everyday basis. When you are working hard for muscle, especially when you use intensity techniques on a regular schedule, you have to pay close attention to ensure you are not creeping into the overtraining state. If you start to feel like you don't want to train, if you feel wired and like you can't sleep or if your resting heart rate increases, these are all signs of overtraining. If you reach that point, you will need to take a few days off. Don't worry – your muscle gains will not disappear in that short time frame, but if you continue training in an overtrained state they will stop and potentially diminish. At the end of this month you will take a scheduled week off as it is – get yourself mentally prepared for this! Now

If you enter into an overtrained state, take a few days off and rest easy. Your gains won't suddenly disappear.

Photo by Paul Buceta
Model: Michael Kefalianos

that you're in the habit of training four times a week and you've been watching your muscles expand you will feel like a slug, with lots of pent-up energy. You can do some active rest during this week – play some basketball, go for walks, ride your bike – but refrain from weight training and don't put too much intense effort into whatever you do. In other words, no hill sprints! You will need this rest to prepare you for the final push to an advanced physique; over the course of months 10, 11 and 12 you will increase your training frequency to six days a week. This increased volume with more exercises in addition to intensity techniques will make months 10 to 12 very challenging.

WEEKS 1 - 2 - 3 - 4
MONDAYS AND THURSDAYS

EXERCISE	SETS	REPS
PRE-EXHAUST FOR CHEST		
Cable Crossover	1	8-12
Flat-Bench Press	3	8-12
Incline Dumbbell Press	3	8-12
PRE-EXHAUST FOR BACK		
Straight-Arm Lat Pushdown	1	8-12
Barbell Row	3	8-12
Lat Pulldown	3	8-12
Front Barbell Press	3	8-12
Bent-Over Lateral Raise	3	8-12
Barbell Shrug	3	8-12
Crunch	3	15-20
Reverse Crunch	3	15-20
External Rotation	2	15-20
Internal Rotation	2	15-20

Photos by Robert Reiff
Model Ben Pakulski

WEEKS 1 – 2 – 3 – 4
TUESDAYS AND FRIDAYS

EXERCISE	SETS	REPS
PRE-EXHAUST FOR QUADS		
Leg Extension	1	8-12
Leg Press	3	8-12
PRE-EXHAUST FOR HAMSTRINGS		
Lying Leg Curl	1	8-12
Stiff-Legged Deadlift	3	8-12
Standing Calf Raise	3	15-20
Seated Calf Raise	3	15-20
EZ-Bar Curl	3	8-12*
Preacher Curl	3	12-15
Lying Triceps Extension	3	8-12*
Cable Pressdown	3	8-12
Wrist Curl	2	15-20
Reverse Wrist Curl	2	15-20

*Negatives on last set – have someone help you bring the barbell up; then complete the repetition yourself
Note: After you complete these four weeks, take one full week off to prepare for the final months of the program.

SUPPLEMENTS
Greens: Get Your Vegetables

High protein is the main theme of body-building diets, and bodybuilders sometimes come up short on other key nutrients when their meal plans are missing adequate amounts of vegetables and fruits. Many individuals consume only a fraction – about one-third, on average – of the suggested daily intake of six to twelve servings of fruits and vegetables. Without consuming enough sources from this food group regularly, individuals are likely to become deficient in micronutrients (vitamins and minerals) that are vital to a wide range of physiological processes. Long-term or severe shortage of sufficient levels of each vitamin and mineral increases an individual's risk of cancer, heart disease, accelerated aging, memory impairment and acid alkaline imbalance, just to name a few. Including a nutrient-rich greens supplement as part of your daily nutrition regimen is an easy and effective way to ensure you are meeting your vegetable and fruit needs.

Greens and Antioxidants

Stress triggers such as environmental toxins, dietary imbalances and lifestyle-related stress all contribute to excessive creation of free radicals in the body. Free-radical production is a natural physiological process that occurs in all humans. The issue, however, is in the quantity of free radicals and, more importantly, how effectively the body can neutralize them. Biochemically free radicals are molecules or atoms that have unpaired electrons or that have lost an electron. Without the electron pair, the molecule becomes unstable, and it seeks out electrons from other molecules within the body. This reactivity becomes a problem because the free radicals can participate in side reactions that cause damage at the cellular level. Unless neutralized, excessive amounts of free radicals can lead to cell injury or death, resulting in many potential conditions and illnesses such as cancer, stroke, disrupted immune function and diabetes.

Antioxidants are one of the body's main defense mechanisms against free radicals. Also molecules, antioxidants work by minimizing the induced free-radical damage and repairing damaged cells. Therefore, the consumption of antioxidant-rich foods is very beneficial and important to good health, and the best whole-food sources are fruits and vegetables. Examples include berries (blueberries, raspberries, blackberries and strawberries), spinach, broccoli, tomatoes and carrots.

Acid/Alkaline (pH) Balance

The foods individuals consume also impact the delicate balance of acids and bases (known as pH balance) in the body. The systems within the body function optimally when the internal environment is neutral to slightly alkaline (with the exception of certain vital organs such as the stomach that produce or house very acidic substances). On the pH scale, intracellular fluid should have a level somewhere in the range of 6.8 to 7.4. If the pH dips and becomes too acidic, enzymes can't function properly and other cellular processes cannot occur. Foods such as meat, sugar, alcohol, coffee and table salt increase acidity. In addition, lifestyle factors such as stress and certain illnesses can throw the pH balance off. Conversely, most fruits and vegetables, as well as all herbs and many different

Certain foods and beverages may increase acidity levels and that can have a direct impact on the functioning ability of enzymes.

Photo by Gregory James
Model Mboya Edwards

124

spices are acid neutralizing, which means they help to restore and maintain the balance of acids and bases. Specific examples of helpful foods include leafy green vegetables, beets, celery, citrus fruits, cherries, figs, along with spices such as cinnamon, curry and ginger.

Whole foods are the best sources of antioxidants and acid-neutralizing compounds, but a quality greens supplement may be beneficial for individuals who find it difficult to include enough fresh fruits and vegetables in their diets. Greens supplements are plant-based compounds manufactured from plant sources such as alfalfa, barley, grains, nuts, spirulina, wheat grass, herbs, vegetables, legumes and seaweed. These supplements are sold in both powder and capsule form. The powder can be added to water or juice and most products are best taken first thing in the morning. Always be sure to read the product label and follow recommended dosage instructions. A single dose of a quality greens formula is equivalent to approximately six to eight servings of fruits and veggies.

Here's a sample daily meal plan for month nine:

Breakfast
- Ham and potato frittata prepared with 1 large whole egg, 5 egg whites, ½ tsp. salt, 1 cup cooked ham (cut into small cubes), 4 tbsp. grated parmesan cheese, 2 tbsp. chopped fresh parsley, 1 cup diced onion, ½ cup chopped zucchini, 1 tbsp. olive oil, ½ cup cherry tomatoes (halved), 2 cups shredded potatoes

Mid-Morning Snack
- Protein shake made with 1 or 2 scoops whey protein powder, water (or low-fat/nonfat milk)
- 2 medium-sized kiwis

Lunch
- Shrimp stir-fry prepared with 6 ounces shrimp, 1½ cups mixed vegetables (e.g., green beans, snow peas, red and yellow pepper, carrots), ¼ cup sodium-reduced soy sauce, 1 clove chopped garlic, 1 tsp. minced ginger, 1 tbsp. olive oil, pepper (to taste)
- 1 cup brown rice

Mid-Afternoon Snack
- Low-fat bran muffin
- 1 medium-sized banana
- Protein shake made with 1 or 2 scoops whey protein powder, water (or low-fat/nonfat milk)

> "Antioxidants work by minimizing the induced free-radical damage and repairing damaged cells. Therefore, the consumption of antioxidant-rich foods is very beneficial and important to good health."

Dinner
- 6 to 8 ounces grilled pork loin
- 1 cup mixed greens with low-fat dressing
- 5 ounces baked yam

Before-Bed Snack
- Protein shake prepared with 1 scoop (approximately 25 grams of protein) casein protein powder, water (or low-fat/nonfat milk)

Photo by Paul Buceta
Model Hidetada Yamagishi

Photo by Gregory James
Model Evgeni Mishin

Photo by Gregory James
Model Toney Freeman

Photo by Michael Butler
Model David Hughes

12

CH.
12

SIX DAYS A WEEK

After your week off from the gym, you should feel especially strong, and you should be chomping at the bit to get training. That feeling is good, because now you'll be training in an entirely new way that will challenge your muscles to the extreme. The final three months of this training program will be very intense and demanding. These routines were designed to simulate how a competitive bodybuilder would train. If you're still relatively new to serious bodybuilding, you may want to consider repeating months seven to nine before transitioning into the advanced program outlined in the next three chapters.

During this phase you will be training six days a week. The increase in workout days means that you will also follow a new bodypart split, with more exercises and sets per bodypart. You will not be doing intensity techniques this month; your intensity will come from the increased frequency and sets.

Your bodypart split will be divided into three groups of main areas: Chest/back, shoulders/arms and legs/abs. You will target each bodypart two different ways each week, for variety and to continue to stimulate the muscles thoroughly.

To continue to stimulate your muscles in month 10, you'll have to begin performing exercises that will attack your bodyparts in fresh new ways.

Photos by Paul Buceta / Gregory James
Models Mike Van Wyck / Michael LiBeratore

WEEKS 1 - 2 - 3 - 4
DAY 1

EXERCISE	SETS	REPS
Flat-Bench Barbell Press	3	8-12
Incline Dumbbell Press	3	8-12
Chest Dip	3	8-12
Bent-Over Barbell Row	3	8-12
T-Bar Row	3	8-12
Seated Row	3	8-12
Wrist Curl	3	12-15
Reverse Wrist Curl	3	12-15
External Rotation	2	15-20
Internal Rotation	2	15-20

WEEKS 1 - 2 - 3 - 4
DAY 2

EXERCISE	SETS	REPS
Front Dumbbell Raise	3	12–15
Cable Lateral Raise	3	12–15
Bent-Over Cable Lateral Raise	3	12–15
Upright Row	3	8–12
Rope Pressdown	3	8–12
Dumbbell Overhead Extension	3	8–12
One-Arm Reverse Cable Extension	3	8–12
Preacher Curl	3	8–12
Dumbbell Concentration Curl	3	8–12
Cable Curl	3	12–15

WEEKS 1 – 2 – 3 – 4
DAY 3

EXERCISE	SETS	REPS
Leg Press	4	8-12
Lunge	3	8-12 (each leg)
Leg Extension	3	12-15
Lying Leg Curl	3	8-12
Stiff-Legged Deadlift	3	8-12
Toe Press	4	12-15
Seated Calf Raise	4	12-15
Reverse Crunch	4	15-20
Knee-In	4	15-20
Medicine Ball Twist	4	15-20

Photo by Paul Buceta
Model Tricky Jackson

Photo by Garry Bartlett
Models D. Wolf, B. Warren, D. Jackson, J. Cutler and P. Heath

WEEKS 1 - 2 - 3 - 4
DAY 4

EXERCISE	SETS	REPS
Push-Up (on Handles)	4	to failure
Incline Dumbbell Flye	3	8-12
Cable Crossover	4	12-15
Chin-Up	1	30 (rest-pause)
One-Arm Row	3	8-12
Straight-Arm Lat Pulldown	4	12-15
Wrist Roller	5	up and down
External Rotation	2	15-20
Internal Rotation	2	15-20

WEEKS 1 - 2 - 3 - 4
DAY 5

EXERCISE	SETS	REPS
Front Barbell Press	3	8-12
Lateral Raise	3	8-12
Reverse Pec-Deck	3	8-12
Shrug	3	8-12
Lying Extension	3	8-12
V-Bar Pressdown	3	8-12
Weighted Bench Dip	3	8-12
Barbell Curl (21s)*	3	21
Alternating Dumbbell Curl	3	8-12
Hammer Curl	3	8-12

*Do the first seven reps over the top half of the range of motion (ROM), the next seven reps over the bottom half of the ROM and the last seven reps over the full ROM.

Photo by Kevin Horton
Model Ed van Amsterdam

WEEKS 1 – 2 – 3 – 4
DAY 6

EXERCISE	SETS	REPS
Squat	5	8-12*
Hack Squat	3	8-12
Deadlift	5	8-12
Seated Leg Curl	3	12-15
Standing Calf Raise	3	15-20
Seated Calf Raise	3	15-20
Captain's Chair *or* Hanging Leg Raise	3	15-20
Twisting Captain's Chair *or* Twisting Hanging Leg Raise	3	15-20
Ab Wheel Rollout	3	8-12

*Do the warm-up sets before your three working sets.

Photo by Kevin Horton
Model Zack Khan

SUPPLEMENTS
VITAMINS AND MINERALS

An individual's body needs more than just the right amounts of protein, carbohydrates and fats to support muscle growth and facilitate strength improvements. You also need to ensure you are getting adequate amounts of vitamins and minerals, or micronutrients, to respond effectively to training. Many bodybuilders stick with standard diets that lack enough variety of whole-food sources. As a result, micronutrient profiles in the body may become unbalanced, which can negatively impact bodybuilding goals.

No single food source provides a satisfactory amount of all the micronutrients, but there are many foods that are rich in certain vitamins and minerals. By consuming a wide range of these superfoods, your body will have the means necessary to encourage tissue growth, support recovery and promote overall health.

For bodybuilders who want to maximize muscular gains, some of the key vitamins and minerals include vitamin C, vitamin E, beta-carotene, zinc and magnesium.

VITAMIN/MINERAL	RECOMMENDED DOSAGE	WHOLE-FOOD SOURCES
Vitamin C	500–2,000 mg per day in supplement form	Orange and grapefruit juice, peaches, sweet red peppers
Vitamin E	400–800 IU per day (with food)	Wheat germ, whole-grain products, dark green leafy vegetables
Beta-Carotene	Up to 5,000 IU (do not take in conjunction with vitamin A, as there is greater risk of toxicity)	Carrot juice, pumpkin, spinach, sweet potato
Zinc	Up to 300 mg (on an empty stomach about 30 minutes before bedtime)	Meats, seafood (especially oysters), eggs, milk
Magnesium	400 mg twice per day (with food)	Whole-grain breads, cereals, pasta noodles and beans

Photo by Michael Butler
Model Mark Dugdale

Certain vitamins and minerals can be dangerous or toxic when levels become too high in the body, so knowing the upper limits for each is very important, especially if you are taking specific micronutrients in supplement form. Some bodybuilders opt for a daily multivitamin/mineral to help ensure they are meeting the minimum requirements for each. The best way to determine whether or not you need a multivitamin as part of your supplement regimen is to critique your diet, assessing the variety you are getting as well as the specific choices you are making for each food group.

Here's a sample daily diet for a cutting or precontest phase:

Breakfast
- 1 cup steel-cut oats
- Spinach and tomato omelet prepared with one whole egg and four egg whites, 1 cup spinach and ½ cup chopped tomato

Mid-Morning Snack
- Protein shake made with 1 or 2 scoops whey protein powder, water

Lunch
- 6 ounces grilled chicken breast
- 1 cup mixed vegetables
- 4 ounces baked yam

Mid-Afternoon Snack
- Protein shake made with 1 or 2 scoops whey protein powder, water

Dinner
- 6 ounces grilled salmon (or other deep-sea fish) or lean red meat
- 2 cups fresh salad
- 1 cup brown rice

Before-Bed Snack
- Omelet prepared with one whole egg and four egg whites

Following this meal plan will get you cut, while at the same time ensuring you get all the necessary vitamins and minerals.

When taking micronutrient supplements it is extremely important that you know your limit and don't exceed it because taking too many could be dangerous.

Photo by Robert Reiff
Model Chris Jalali

Photo by Gregory James
Model Joel Thomas and Andy Haman

Photo by Paul Buceta
Model Essa Obaid

Photo by Gregory James
Model Blair Mone

Photo by Michael Butler
Model Keith Williams

GETTING LEAN AND RIPPED

13

CH.
13

GETTING LEAN AND RIPPED

During month 10 you increased the intensity and frequency of your training split and you modified your diet slightly, gearing it toward shedding bodyfat and getting cut. Before you start into this month's program, it is important to review the last four weeks and assess how your body is responding. Be aware of any symptoms of overtraining – you want to avoid sending your body into a catabolic (muscle-wasting) state. The goal over these final few months is to get lean and ripped while still preserving all your hard-earned muscle mass. Make minor adjustments to your training routine or nutrition plan, if necessary.

After 10 months of training you're just about ready to show off your massive muscle gains. Now's the time to get lean and ripped!

Your goal may finally seem within reach, but to succeed in your quest you'll still need to assess and possibly fine-tune your training.

Photos by Rich Baker / Garry Bartlett
Model Phil von Kaenel / Dexter Jackson

WEEKS 1 - 2 - 3 - 4
DAYS 1 AND 4

EXERCISE	SETS	REPS
Incline-Bench Barbell Press	3-4	8-12
Flat-Bench Dumbbell Flye	3-4	8-12
Parallel-Bar Dip	3-4	8-12 (to failure)
Dumbbell Overhead Press *triset with*	3-4	8-12
Dumbbell Lateral Raise	3-4	8-12
Upright Row	3-4	8-12
Barbell Shrug	3-4	8-12
Internal Rotation	2	20
External Rotation	2	20

WEEKS 1 - 2 - 3 - 4
DAYS 2 AND 5

EXERCISE	SETS	REPS
Front Lat Pulldown *superset with*	3-4	8-12
Reverse-Grip Lat Pulldown	3-4	8-12
One-Arm Dumbbell Row	3-4	8-12
Preacher Curl	3-4	8-12
Standing Dumbbell Curl	3-4*	8-12
Incline Dumbbell Curl	3-4	8-12
Skullcrusher *superset with*	3-4	8-12
Narrow-Grip Bench Press	3-4	8-12
Reverse One-Arm Cable Extension	3-4	8-12

*Perform a drop set on the last set.

WEEKS 1 - 2 - 3 - 4
DAYS 3 AND 6

EXERCISE	SETS	REPS
Leg Extension *pre-exhaust with*	3-4	8-12
Leg Press	3-4	8-12
Hack Squat	3-4	8-12
Lying Leg Curl *triset with*	3-4	8-12
Seated Leg Curl	3-4	8-12
Stiff-Legged Deadlift	3-4	8-12
Standing Calf Raise	3-4	15-20
Seated Calf Raise	3-4	15-20
Swiss Ball Crunch*	10	10

*Perform this exercise with the 10x10 method, resting no more than one minute between sets.

SUPPLEMENTS
L-Glutamine

Glutamine is a free-form amino acid that is abundant within the body and in most protein-rich foods. It is an important amino acid intermediate to a number of internal processes, so it's in high demand and resides everywhere in the body. It is classified as a conditionally essential amino acid; the body can synthesize an adequate amount to meet physiological needs under normal circumstances, but when an individual's body is subjected to physical stress (e.g., trauma, illnesses such as cancer, intense exercise or dieting) it may not be able to synthesize enough. Under these conditions, L-glutamine becomes an essential amino acid, and it is therefore very important to consume sufficient amounts to meet the increased physiological demands created by these situations.

For bodybuilders, glutamine is regarded as one of the most important amino acids when the body is under conditions of stress. Glutamine is the predominant amino acid in skeletal muscle, and both the digestive and immune systems use this amino acid to help maintain health. In skeletal muscle, glutamine is crucial for protein synthesis. During heavy exercise, however, it gets depleted so individuals need to consume adequate amounts to prevent muscle-tissue breakdown. Studies have demonstrated glutamine

supplementation can boost muscular growth and reduce catabolism, especially for bodybuilders who are undergoing calorie restriction. Furthermore, glutamine supplementation has been scientifically proven to increase muscle cell volume and increase growth-hormone release.

The standard dose of supplemental glutamine for bodybuilders and other athletes is 5 grams taken before and after training.

Here's a sample daily diet for month 11. This is still a pre-contest diet with reduced carbohydrates. If you find that you're becoming weak, add a piece of fruit or sweet potato.

Breakfast
- 1 whole egg
- 5 egg whites
- 1 cup cream of wheat

Mid-Morning Snack
- Protein shake made with 1 or 2 scoops whey protein powder, water

Lunch
- 6 to 8 ounces grilled turkey breast
- 1 cup raw vegetables
- 1 slice whole-grain bread

Mid-Afternoon Snack
- Protein shake made with 1 or 2 scoops whey protein powder, water

Dinner
- 8 to 10 ounces grilled tilapia
- 1 cup mixed greens
- 1 medium baked yam

Before-Bed Snack
- Protein shake prepared with 1 scoop (approximately 25 grams of protein) casein protein powder, water

When you force your body through intense physical stress, glutamine levels become depleted. Muscle-tissue breakdown may occur.

Photo by Ralph DeHaan
Model Mark Dugdale

Photo by Michael Butler
Model David Hughes

Photo by Jason Breeze
Model Marlon John

Photo by Jason Breeze
Model Mark Richman

Photo by Ralph DeHaan
Model David Henry

THE FINAL COUNTDOWN

14

CH. 14

Photo by Gregory James
Model: Branden Curry

THE FINAL COUNTDOWN

In this final month of the program, you will make a minor adjustment to your six-day training split. During months 10 and 11 you trained six days in a row, taking every seventh day off. This month, however, you will follow a three-days-on/one-day-off split, so you will perform the first workout on days 1 and 5, the second on days 2 and 6, and the third on days 3 and 7. Days 4 and 8 will be rest days.

Through this journey you've learned a new way of life, but more importantly you've emerged as a new person with massive muscles and self-confidence.

Photos by Paul Buceta / Kevin Horton
Model Fouad Abiad / Ed van Amsterdam

WEEKS 1 – 2 – 3 – 4
DAYS 1 AND 5

EXERCISE	SETS	REPS
Squat	3–4	8–12
Leg Press	3–4	8–12
Lying Leg Curl *superset with*	3–4	8–12
Stiff-Legged Deadlift	3–4	8–12
Standing Calf Raise *triset with*	3–4	8–12
Seated Calf Raise	3–4	8–12
Toe Press (on leg press)	3–4	8–12

WEEKS 1 – 2 – 3 – 4
DAYS 2 AND 6

EXERCISE	SETS	REPS
Cable Crossover *triset with*	3–4	8–12
Flat-Bench Dumbbell Press	3–4	8–12
Incline-Bench Dumbbell Flye	3–4	8–12
Chin-Up	1–2	30*
Seated Cable Row	3–4	8–12
Standing One-Arm Cable Row	3–4	8–12
Back Extension	3–4	15–20
Plank	3–4	to failure

*Use rest-pause to reach 30 reps in total per set.

Photos by Paul Buceta / Gregory James
Models Evgeni Mishin and Catherine Holland / Marcus Haley

Photo by Paul Buceta
Model Eduardo Corrêa da Silva

WEEKS 1 - 2 - 3 - 4
DAYS 3 AND 7

EXERCISE	SETS	REPS
Seated Dumbbell Press	3-4	8-12
Dumbbell Lateral Raise	3-4	8-12
Bent-Over Lateral Raise	3-4	8-12
Upright Row	3-4	8-12
EZ-Bar Curl	3-4	8-12
Incline Curl	3-4	8-12
Concentration Curl	3-4	8-12
Dumbbell Extension	3-4	8-12
Bench Dip	3-4	8-12
Rope Pressdown	3-4	8-12
Hanging Leg Raise	3-4	15-20
Reverse Crunch triset with	3-4	15-20+
Swiss Ball Crunch	3-4	15-20+
Oblique Crunch	3-4	15-20+

*Take days 4 and 8 off.

SUPPLEMENTS
Meal-Replacement Powders

Meal-replacement powders, or MRPs, are prepackaged drink mixes that you combine with water, milk or juice and consume in place of a meal (or as a snack in addition to whole-food meals). MRPs have a balanced nutritional profile, containing all the key nutrients, vitamins and minerals that you would otherwise get from a whole-food meal. With MRPs, however, you get all the nutrition in a fast and convenient beverage. In fact, most products on the market contain more than 100 percent of the U.S. reference dietary intake of every essential vitamin and mineral. MRPs are high in protein and low in fat; there are also low-carb options as well as MRPs with a good balance of protein and complex carbs. For bodybuilders, MRPs can be a beneficial tool because they're convenient, can be mixed easily and are so nutrient dense. Research has also shown certain MRPs can boost metabolism.

Flaxseed oil is sometimes used to fortify MRPs with essential fatty acids. Certain products may also contain complex carbs from sources such as oats, whole wheat, maltodextrin and brown rice. Other ingredients in MRPs can include amino acids, herbal additives and other muscle-building ingredients.

Before choosing a specific MRP product, do some research on the contents and ingredients, as there are various options. Some types are higher in calories (for offseason) and some varieties are calorie-reduced (for precontest/cutting phase). Look for products that contain a combination of whey, milk and egg proteins as the first ingredients. You should also select a product that has fewer than 300 calories (when taken with water), contains at least 40 grams of protein and has minimal fat (when you are not in a gaining phase).

Here is a sample daily meal plan for month 12, your final cutting month.

Breakfast
- 1 cup cream of rice
- 1 whole egg
- 5 egg whites

> "MRPs are high in protein and low in fat; there are also low-carb options as well as MRPs with a good balance of protein and complex carbs."

Mid-Morning Snack
- Protein shake made with 1 or 2 scoops whey protein powder, water

Lunch
- 7 ounces grilled Atlantic cod fillet
- 1 cup steamed broccoli and cauliflower
- 1 medium baked yam

Mid-Afternoon Snack
- Protein shake made with 1 or 2 scoops whey protein powder, water

Dinner
- Honey Dijon pork prepared with 7 ounces pork tenderloin, 1 tbsp. Dijon mustard, 1 tbsp. honey, 2 tsp. lemon juice, salt and pepper (to taste)
- 2 cups spinach salad
- 1 cup brown rice

Before-Bed Snack
- 1 cup cottage cheese mixed with ½–1 scoop casein protein powder

Photo by Kevin Horton
Model Alvin Small

ADVANCED TRAINING TECHNIQUES

CHEAT REPS/CHEATING TECHNIQUE

Cheating is a technique that involves using loose form as a way to get a few extra reps beyond failure within the target range in a set. Bodybuilders can use other muscles to assist in generating momentum or a bit of body English to get past a sticking point. For the cheating principle to be effective, make sure you incorporate it only after the primary muscles have failed. If you need to cheat from the first rep, or from any rep within the designated range for that set, you're using too much weight.

There's a correct and an incorrect way to cheat. A slight loosening of form is acceptable, but poor form will put you at increased risk of injury and will serve no benefit to your muscles. One of the worst mistakes to make while cheating is bouncing the weight up. Bouncing at the top or bottom of a move places undue stress on the body's soft connective tissues. For example, one of the most common errors bodybuilders make when performing the bench press is bouncing the weight off their chests, which can damage the ribcage and decrease the effectiveness of the movement.

The key to effective cheating is knowing when and how to cheat. Do not use cheat reps excessively in your workout. Choose one exercise and at the end of a set when you can't do any more reps with good form, use a bit of swing or momentum to get a few extra reps. Remember, cheating is meant to work the muscle harder, not to make the exercise easier.

PARTIAL REPS OR "BURNS"

Partial reps were first popularized in bodybuilding by training guru Vince Gironda. Instead of moving the weight through a full range of motion (ROM), partial reps are performed over only part of the ROM. Quite often this technique is used either on the top half or bottom half of the ROM, so the full range is split into two sections. Partial reps can also be used effectively at the end of a given set to extend it – the weight should remain the same and you gradually continue to shorten the range of motion as your muscles become more exhausted. For example, if you can manage 10 reps (over the full range of motion) of a barbell curl, instead of stopping the set at the 10th rep, curl the bar up as far as you can to squeeze out a few more reps. Even if you can curl the bar only 6 to 8 inches, extending the set in this fashion is beneficial because you're still hitting muscle fibers you wouldn't have if you'd ended the set at the 10th rep.

ULTRASLOW REPS

Most bodybuilders take 3 to 5 seconds to complete a rep. This range is fast enough to use a decent amount of weight, and yet slow enough to keep the muscle under tension for 30 to 50 seconds (using 10 reps as an example). But to add variety you can choose to experiment with ultraslow reps in which you take anywhere from 10 to 30 seconds to complete one rep.

Ultraslow training offers a number of benefits. For starters, it eliminates almost all body momentum – and thus cheating. Lifting and lowering a weight in ultraslow motion takes pure muscle power. Another advantage is safety. Most injuries come from a combination of lifting too much weight too fast. Such abrupt stopping and starting can damage the tendons, ligaments and muscles. Ultraslow training eliminates virtually all of these dangerous actions. Also keep in mind that lifting a weight using 10- to

30-second reps requires much lighter poundage. On the surface this may sound counterproductive, but don't forget you'll strictly be using muscle power, not momentum, to lift the lighter weight. Slowly lifting the weight will force you to really focus on the task at hand. Most bodybuilders who employ this technique find that they're able to lift the weight through a greater range of motion.

STRIP SETS

Strip sets are both simple to do and produce outstanding results. This technique is performed with a barbell, in which, as the name suggests, you literally "strip" the weight off the bar when you reach failure (you're unable to perform another rep).

For example, say you're using 200 pounds on the bench press for 10 reps; once you fail on the 10th rep, quickly rack the bar and remove 20 or 25 pounds (instead of taking your normal rest period). Your chest, triceps and shoulder muscles may not be able to handle 200 pounds, but no doubt they're capable of continuing with 175 to 180 pounds for a few more reps. You could keep removing weight until you're left with just the bar, but most bodybuilders just do two or three drops.

21s

This technique is so named because of the number of reps you do during the set. While they can be performed on most exercises they're most suited to curling movements – particularly barbell curls. Grab a barbell and curl the bar from the bottom to the halfway point (i.e. your forearm is parallel with the floor). Do this for seven reps. Then curl the bar all the way up to the top and lower to the halfway point for seven more reps. Lastly lower the bar to

your thighs and complete seven full barbell curls.

After one set of 21s you'll discover that you can't use your normal workout poundage – partial movements force the biceps to work just as hard, if not harder, than straight sets with heavier weight.

STAGGERED SETS

A staggered set is when you perform an exercise for one bodypart and then immediately perform a set of an exercise for a different bodypart. For example, while training your chest you can slip in a set of calf raises between each of your chest exercises or do forearm work between leg exercises.

You'll notice that I suggested doing calves with chest, or other upper body exercises, and forearms with leg work. There's a reason for this. You need your calves for stabilizing on most leg exercises, and your forearms play a big role in training the upper body. If you train forearms between chest or back exercises, you won't be able to lift the same amount of weight or complete the regular number of reps. Keep this in mind when deciding which bodyparts you're going to perform staggered sets with.

NEGATIVE REPS

There's been a great deal of research to suggest that the negative part of an exercise (the eccentric or contraction to rest) is just as productive as the positive portion (concentric or rest to contraction). Negative-only training received a big endorsement from Dr. Arthur Jones, inventor of the Nautilus line of strength-training equipment.

There are two ways to perform negatives. The first is to lower the weight in the same slow and controlled manner as you raise it. In other words, you're not just hoisting the weight into position and letting gravity pull it down; instead you're using muscle power to keep the weight under control. An example of this is the lowering of the weight to the chest during a bench press.

The other way is to load more weight on the bar than you can normally lift and then lower it as slowly as possible, trying to stop the weight on the way down. For example, on the barbell bench press you'd have a training partner help you push the bar to the top of the movement, and then slowly lower it using your chest, shoulder and triceps muscles.

> "Pre-exhaustion means you first fatigue or 'pre-exhaust' the primary muscles with an isolation exercise and then perform a compound movement."

You can also do negatives on your own on a few exercises. For example, on the barbell curl you'd curl the weight up using body momentum and then slowly lower it using just the biceps. You can do the same thing on various lateral raises for shoulders.

I GO YOU GO

This training principle is virtually guaranteed to shock your muscles to new growth because of the high level of intensity. As the name suggests it involves having one partner perform a set of a given exercise and then passing the dumbbells or barbell to the other partner who then trains to failure. You go back and forth training to failure with no break in between sets. Because of the sheer intensity of the

technique, it's best limited to smaller muscles like arms and shoulders.

REST-PAUSE

Rest-pause is an advanced training technique that separates the true bodybuilders from the wussies! This technique allows you to get more reps than usual with the same weight. To perform rest-pause, load a bar (or machine) with enough weight to limit you to just one rep. Perform the rep and then place the bar back on the rack. Wait 10 to 15 seconds and then do another rep. Repeat this pattern for 8 to 10 reps. Rest-pause is based on the principle that a muscle will regain most of its strength in as little as 10 to 15 seconds. It's also a great technique for blasting through sticking points because you're using 100 percent of your one-rep maximum weight on every set. If you find that you can only squeeze out 5 or 6 reps with the weight, reduce it by about 10 percent.

PRE-EXHAUST

We have Robert Kennedy, publisher of *MuscleMag International*, to thank for this one. He's penned over 50 books and thousands of magazine articles, making it safe to declare him an expert on building great physiques. Bob came up with the pre-exhaust training principle back in 1968. This technique is great for eliminating the "weak link" that often limits the effectiveness of many otherwise great exercises.

Pre-exhaustion means you first fatigue or "pre-exhaust" the primary muscles with an isolation exercise and then perform a compound movement that let's the now stronger secondary muscles carry the targeted muscle to new depths of stimulation.

For example many bodybuilders find that barbell presses do more for their triceps and front shoulders than their chest. This is because these smaller muscles often tire before the larger chest muscles. To avoid this, first perform an isolation exercise, such as flat-bench dumbbell flyes or pec-deck flyes, and then do a set of barbell presses. The flyes will target just the chest muscles, leaving the triceps and shoulders relatively fresh. Then when you switch to the barbell bench press, the chest muscles are now the "weak link" and will tire and fatigue before the still-energized triceps and front shoulders do.

SUPERSETS

They're quick, fun and very efficient. Supersets involve performing two exercises in an alternating fashion, but rather than waiting the usual 45 to 60 seconds between exercises your rest is only as long as it takes to switch from one exercise to the next.

There are two primary versions of supersets. The first involves alternating two exercises for the same muscle group; for example, a set of flat-bench barbell presses followed by a set of incline dumbbell flyes. Or you could alternate incline barbell presses with dips. Most bodybuilders try to superset exercises that hit the muscle from different angles or different parts of the muscle. For example: lower and upper chest, inner and outer back, and front and rear shoulders.

The second variation of supersets involves alternating two exercises for different muscle groups. There are no hard rules but since most of the body's major muscles work in pairs, most bodybuilders tend to superset exercises for opposing muscle groups such as back and chest, quads and hamstrings, and biceps and triceps. At right are some great examples of both superset variations.

SUPERSETS FOR THE SAME MUSCLE GROUPS

QUADS
Leg Extension	Squat
Hack Squat	Leg Press

HAMSTRINGS
Lying Leg Curl	Stiff-Legged Deadlift
Stiff-Legged Deadlift	Seated Leg Curl

CHEST
Flat-Bench Flye	Barbell Bench Press
Incline Dumbbell Press	Incline Dumbbell Flye
Flat-Bench Dumbbell Press	Dip

BACK
Straight-Arm Pushdown	Front Pulldown
Chin-Up	Barbell Row
Seated Row	T-Bar Row

SHOULDERS
Side Dumbbell Raise	Dumbbell Press
Front Dumbbell Raise	Upright Row

BICEPS
Incline Curl	Standing Barbell Curl
Preacher Curl	Narrow Reverse Chin-Up

TRICEPS
Lying Extension	Narrow Press
Triceps Pushdown	Dip

ABS
Swiss Ball Crunch	Reverse Crunch
Hanging Leg Raise	Medicine Ball Twist

CALVES
Standing Calf Raise	Seated Calf Raise
Donkey Calf Raise	Seated Calf Raise
Seated Calf Raise	Toe Press

SUPERSETS FOR OPPOSING MUSCLE GROUPS

QUADS & HAMSTRINGS

Leg Press	Stiff-Legged Deadlift
Squat	Lying Leg Curl
Leg Extension	Seated Leg Curl

CHEST & BACK

Flat-Bench Barbell Press	Chin-Up
Incline Dumbbell Press	Seated Row
Flat-Bench Dumbbell Flye	Front Pulldown

BICEPS & TRICEPS

Barbell Curl	Lying Barbell Extension
Incline Dumbbell Curl	Two-Arm Dumbbell Extension
Preacher Curl	Triceps Pushdown

ABS & LOWER BACK

Swiss Ball Crunch	Back Extension
Reverse Crunch	Stiff-Legged Deadlift

TRI-SETS

As soon as bodybuilders started putting two exercises together, back to back, it was only a matter of time before someone started alternating three different movements. Tri-sets are great for shocking the muscles and allowing you to hit them from every conceivable angle. Like supersets, they also save you time.

TRI-SET COMBOS

QUADS

1. Squat	2. Leg Press	3. Leg Extension

HAMSTRINGS

1. Stiff-Legged Deadlift	2. Lying Leg Curl	3. Seated Leg Curl

CHEST

1. Flat-Bench Barbell Press	2. Incline Dumbbell Press	3. Dip
1. Incline Dumbbell Flye	2. Dip	3. Cable Crossover

BACK

1. Chin-Up	2. T-Bar Row	3. Front Pulldown
1. Barbell Row	2. Narrow Pulldown	3. Seated Cable Row

SHOULDERS

1. Side Dumbbell Raise	2. Dumbbell Press	3. Reverse Pec-Deck

BICEPS

1. Preacher Curl	2. Hammer Curl	3. Incline Dumbbell Curl

TRICEPS

1. Lying Triceps Extension	2. Narrow Press	3. Bench Dip

ABS

1. Swiss Ball Crunch	2. Reverse Crunch	3. Medicine Ball Twist
1. Hanging Leg Raise	2. Floor Crunch	3. Ball Pass

CALVES

1. Standing Calf Raise	2. Seated Calf Raise	3. Toe Press

GIANT SETS

Nothing too complicated here. Instead of putting three exercises together you combine four or more movements for the same muscle group. I caution you that giant sets are a very intense form of training and you won't want to do more than two or three giant sets for bigger muscles and one or two for smaller. In fact, since the arms will be getting a good deal of stimulation from training the chest, back and shoulders, you'll probably only need to do one giant set.

GIANT SET COMBOS

QUADS

1. Squat	2. Leg Press	3. Leg Extension	4. Hack Squat
1. Lunge	2. Sissy Squat	3. Leg Extension	4. Smith-Machine Squat

HAMSTRINGS

1. Lying Leg Curl	2. Seated Leg Curl	3. Stiff-Legged Deadlift	4. Back Extension

CALVES

1. Toe Press	2. Standing Calf Raise	3. Seated Calf Raise	4. Donkey Calf Raise

CHEST

1. Flat-Bench Barbell Press	2. Incline Dumbbell Press	3. Flat-Bench Dumbbell Flye	4. Dip
1. Incline Dumbbell Press	2. Flat-Bench Dumbbell Flye	3. Dip	4. Cable Crossover

BACK

1. Chin-Up	2. T-Bar Row	3. Front Pulldown	4. Barbell Row
1. Seated Row	2. Front Pulldown	3. T-Bar Row	4. Reverse-Grip Chin-Up

SHOULDERS

1. Dumbbell Press	2. Side Dumbbell Raise	3. Reverse Pec-Deck	4. Upright Row
1. Barbell Press	2. Side Cable Raise	3. Bent-Over Lateral Raise	4. Barbell Shrug

BICEPS

1. Preacher Curl	2. Incline Dumbbell Curl	3. Standing Dumbbell Curl	4. Hammer Curl
1. Barbell Curl	2. Standing Dumbbell Curl	3. Cable Curl	4. Preacher Curl

TRICEPS

1. Lying Barbell Extension	2. Narrow Press	3. Bench Dip	4. Two-Arm Dumbbell Extension
1. Triceps Pushdown	2. Lying Dumbbell Extension	3. Behind-The-Head Cable Extension	4. Machine Pushdown

ABS

1. Hanging Leg Raise	2. Swiss Ball Crunch	3. Reverse Crunch	4. Medicine Ball Twist
1. Ball Pass	2. Plank	3. Swiss Ball Crunch	4. Lying Leg Raise

Photo by Paul Buceta
Model Fouad Abiad

EXTENDED SETS

Although some of the previous techniques seem to be more popular, extended sets place second to none when it comes to increasing training intensity and muscle size. To perform extended sets, first carry an exercise to positive failure and then immediately switch to an exercise that puts you in a better biomechanical position. For example, after doing lying barbell extensions quickly bring the bar to your mid-chest and rep out with narrow presses.

Another useful combination is dumbbell flyes and dumbbell presses. Start with the dumbbell flye, then when you can no longer continue, rotate your hands and continue with dumbbell presses. You're stronger in the press than the flye since the press brings in more of the triceps and front shoulders. In effect, you're using these still-fresh muscles to stimulate the chest muscles deeper than if you'd terminated the set with the flyes. You can do the flye/press combination for both flat and incline versions.

Still another great extended set combination is wide and narrow pulldowns. After going to failure on the front pulldown, switch to the narrow, reverse-grip pulldown. The underhand grip brings more of the biceps into play and allows you to push the lats past the normal failure point.

For a great deltoid workout try doing side dumbbell raises followed by dumbbell presses. Although you'll usually be able to lift more weight on the pressing movement, doing the side raises first will tire out the shoulders and odds are you won't need to use heavier dumbbells.

Nothing blasts the biceps like incline dumbbell curls followed by standing barbell curls. Although both exercises work the biceps, the standing curl brings in more forearms and allows you to lift more weight. If you really want to maximize the biceps, add a few cheat curls at the end of your barbell curls. It won't take many sets of this dynamic combo to pack some muscle on your upper arms.

If you're looking to shock the quads into new growth, try the front and back squat extended set combination. Front squats reduce the amount of lower back and glute involvement and are more isolating for the quads. As soon as they're fatigued from the front squats, rack the bar, step under it and perform as many reps as possible of regular back squats. The still strong lower back and glutes will push the quads to new depths of stimulation (and pain).

You can even do extended sets for the abs. Start with crunches on the Swiss ball or floor and once the abs are sufficiently fatigued switch over to reverse crunches. Reverse crunches allow you to use the hip flexors to continue working the abs.

As with most advanced training techniques it's easy to go overboard with extended sets. For most intermediate bodybuilders, one to two extended set combinations will be more than enough. Any more and you risk overtraining.

10X10 (10 SETS OF 10), GERMAN VOLUME TRAINING

There are numerous advantages to training a muscle using multiple exercises during one workout. The most important is that you can attack the muscle from a variety of different angles. The more angles you hit the muscle from, the more muscle fibers stimulated and the greater the overall degree of development. For example, on chest you can do declines for the lower and outer chest, flats for the lower and center chest, inclines for the upper chest, and pec-deck flyes and cable crossovers for the inner chest.

Another advantage of multiple exercises is variety. Even though most bodybuilders love training, doing the same workout repeatedly can get pretty boring. Changing the exercises keeps the routine fresh.

If there's one disadvantage to multiple exercises, however, it's that it's very easy to fall into the overtraining trap. Take shoulders for example. If you were to do one exercise for each of the three heads, plus another exercise for the trapezius, you'd end up doing 12 to 16 sets in total (assuming 3 to 4 sets per exercise). The average natural bodybuilder will quickly overtrain doing that many.

One solution to this is to adopt a one-exercise-per-bodypart-per-workout approach. The technique was first made popular as 10 sets of 10 by California's Vince Gironda in the 1950s and '60s. (In the 1970s it was renamed "German volume training.")

> "A couple of minutes may not seem like a long time, but sometimes it's long enough for the muscles to cool down."

As the name suggests, you pick just one exercise for a muscle and perform 10 sets of 10 reps. Obviously you won't be able to do this with the amount of weight you'd peak at for 3 or 4 sets. In most cases you'll be lucky to use 50 percent. Don't let the first few sets mislead you. They may feel easy but by the time you're up to set 7 or 8 the muscle will be howling! You'll be lucky to complete the 10 full reps on the last couple of sets.

There are numerous advantages to performing just one exercise per body-part. The most obvious is that once you start your entire focus is kept on that one exercise for the full 10 sets. Another benefit is that you won't have to worry about cooling down while changing exercises. This is especially true during busy times when you may have to wait five or ten minutes to get access to a piece of equipment. In the case of barbell exercises, even if there's one free, you'll still have to set it up on a rack and load on the plates. A couple of minutes may not seem like a long time, but sometimes it's long enough for the muscles to cool down. By doing just one exercise you'll never be more than 45 to 60 seconds between sets.

A third advantage to doing just one exercise lies in thoroughness. It usually takes two or three sets before the muscles even feel like they're working. With multiple exercise routines you may complete the first exercise and not even feel it. But if you're doing just one exercise you know it won't be long before the muscles start burning from that particular movement.

Some readers may be concerned about the lack of variety if you're only performing one exercise per workout. To prevent this, simply switch exercises every workout or so. For example, you could do flat-bench barbell presses during one workout, incline dumbbell presses the next and dips on the third (tough to do as your bodyweight may eventually be too heavy to complete the last couple of sets). By alternating the exercises you're still hitting the muscle from different angles – just not during the same workout.

The following table consists of three sample workouts that you can perform for each bodypart. You can still follow your traditional muscle group splits (i.e. three, four or six days per week) but you do only one exercise per bodypart. This means that your total workout for any given day is going to be only two or three exercises.

THREE-DAY BODYPART TRAINING

MUSCLE	DAY 1	DAY 2	DAY 3
Quads	Leg Press	Squats	Hack Squat
Hamstrings	Seated Leg Curl	Standing Leg Curl	Stiff-Legged Deadlift
Calves	Standing Calf Raise	Toe Press	Seated Calf Raise
Chest	Flat-Bench Barbell Press	Incline Dumbbell Press	Dip
Back	Chin-Up	Barbell Row	Seated Cable Row
Shoulders	Dumbbell Press	Bent-Over Raise	Side Dumbbell Raise
Biceps	Barbell Curl	Preacher Curl	Incline Dumbbell Curl
Triceps	Lying Extension	Bench Dip	Cable Pushdown
Abs	Swiss Ball Crunch	Reverse Crunch	Hanging Leg Raise

Photo by Kevin Horton
Model Markus Rühl

EXERCISE DESCRIPTIONS

ABDOMINALS

CRUNCH

You'll need a flat bench or chair to perform this exercise. Lie down on the floor and rest your calves on the bench. Adjust your distance from the bench so your thighs are perpendicular to the floor. Now contract through your abs to lift your shoulders and upper back off the floor. Hold for a second and then slowly lower to the start.

COMMENTS – Most bodybuilders consider crunches one of the best abdominal builders. At first you may want to perform the movement with your hands by your sides. As you get stronger, place your hands to the side of your head, which will add the weight of the arms to your upper body, thus making the exercise more difficult.

MUSCLES WORKED – Crunches primarily work the upper abs, but there's also some lower ab stimulation. The exercise also brings the hip abductors into play.

REVERSE CRUNCH

Lie back on the floor with your hands under your head. Lift your legs off the floor and bend your knees to form a 90-degree angle. Slowly draw your knees toward your chest, lifting your glutes and hips off the floor. Return to the start.

COMMENTS – To reduce the stress on the lower back don't allow the legs to reach a full locked-out position.

MUSCLES WORKED – Reverse crunches primarily work the lower abs but the obliques, lower back, intercostals and upper abs also come into play.

SWISS BALL CRUNCH

Sit on the ball and slowly walk your feet forward, lying back so that the ball is positioned in the natural curve of your lower back. From here the movement is virtually identical to the floor crunch. With your hands behind your head, elbows pointing straight out and eyes focused on the ceiling, slowly crunch your torso towards your pelvis. Slowly return to the starting position so your torso is just below the horizontal.

COMMENTS – The two primary advantages of ball crunches is that they allow you to exercise the abs through a slightly greater range of motion and they force the smaller core muscles to contract for stabilizing purposes.

MUSCLES WORKED – Ball crunches primarily work the upper abs as well as the lower abs, obliques, lower back and intercostals.

MEDICINE BALL TWIST

Sit on the floor with your legs out in front and a slight bend at the knees. Holding a medicine ball at your upper chest, lean back, slowly twist to one side and then back to the center for a one-second pause. Twist to the other side and again back to the center. Repeat.

COMMENTS – To make this exercise more challenging, raise one foot off the ground. You could perform 15 to 20 reps and then switch legs, or alternate the feet every 4 or 5 reps. When raising one foot becomes easy, try performing the exercise with both feet off the ground.

MUSCLES WORKED – Medicine ball twists work the upper and lower abs as well as the intercostals and obliques.

LEG RAISE

Lie down on the abdominal board. Grasp the handgrip behind your head. Bend your legs slightly and lift them toward the ceiling until they're just short of perpendicular. Pause a second and then slowly lower them to the start. Try not to let your feet touch at the bottom, in order to keep the tension on the abdominals throughout the exercise.

COMMENTS – Once again, don't perform the movement with straight legs. Also,

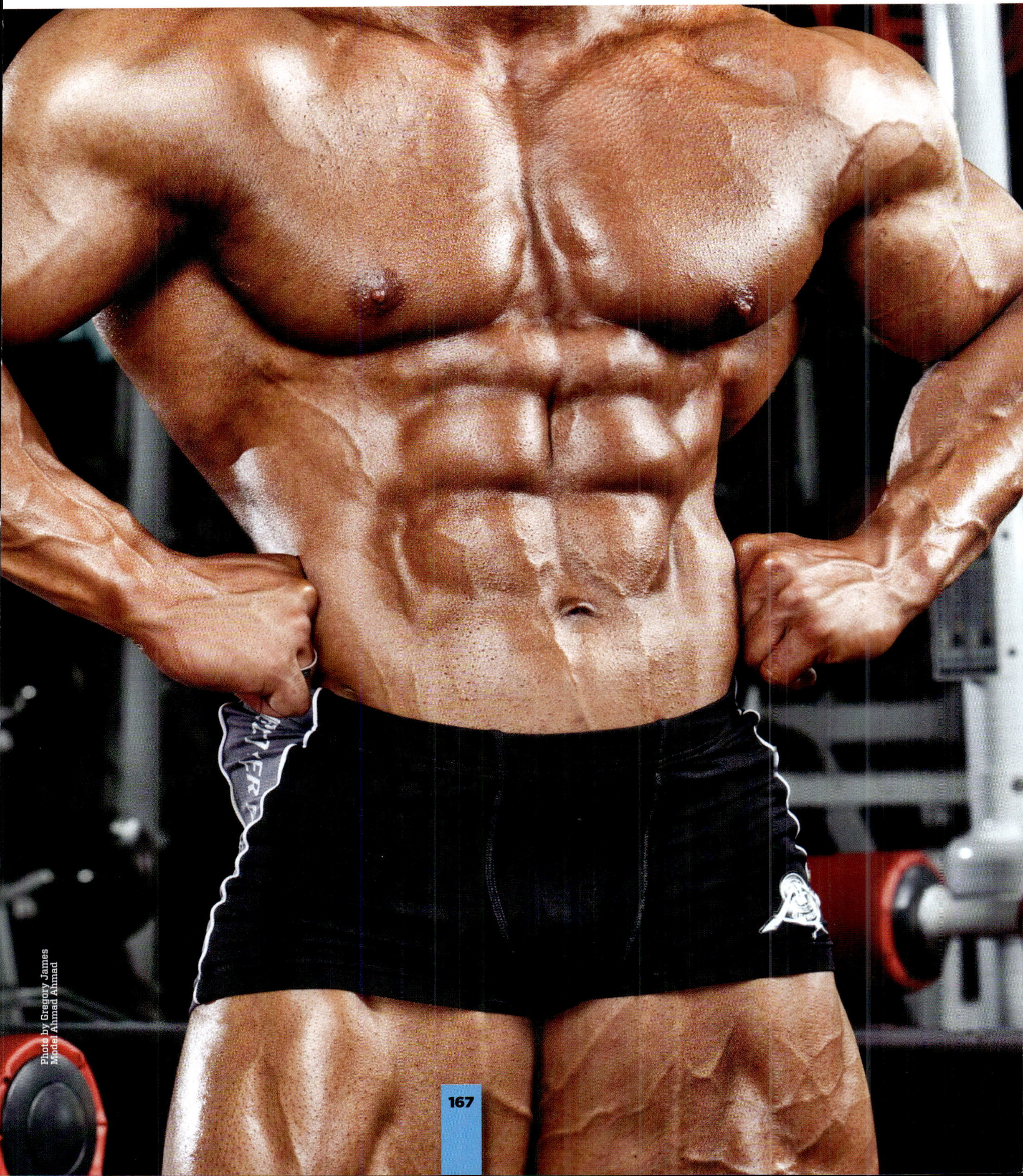

Photo by Gregory James
Model Ahmad Ahmad

resist the urge to use your upper body to pull your legs up. Use only abdominal strength. Start with the abdominal board in the lowest position, and as you get stronger you can increase the angle, thus making the exercise more difficult.

MUSCLES WORKED – Leg raises primarily work the lower abdominals, but the upper abs and hip abductors also come into play.

ROPE CRUNCH

Kneel down facing a high-pulley cable with a rope attached. Grasp the ends of the rope so that it's straddling your neck (i.e. one side of the rope touching each ear). With your knees and feet kept firmly on the ground, bend forward until your forehead is a couple of inches from the floor. Hold this position and flex your abs for a second before slowly returning to the start.

COMMENTS – This is one of the hardest exercises to master as the body tries to cheat by rocking the torso up and down. Even with good technique, some get nothing out of this exercise while others find they have to tire their abs with another exercise before benefiting from rope crunches.

MUSCLES WORKED – Rope crunches work the entire abdominal region and the hip flexors.

PLANK

Lie facedown on the floor, resting on your forearms. Rise off the floor and support your body on your toes and forearms. With your body kept straight from head to heels, try to hold the movement for as long as you can. Resist the urge to raise your butt.

COMMENTS – Planks are among the most misleading ab exercises. In the first 10 to 20 seconds you may think they're not doing much, but that quickly changes. Before long your abs and spi-

nal erectors are screaming for mercy. Try to hold it for a minute or longer and attempt a few more seconds in your next set.

MUSCLES WORKED – Planks target virtually the entire core region – upper and lower abdominals, obliques and spinal erectors. They also force you to use just about every other muscle for stabilization.

CAPTAIN'S CHAIR or HANGING LEG RAISE

With your feet together and your legs as straight as possible, begin by using your hands to hang off an overhead bar. Lift your legs as high as possible, remembering to keep them fairly straight throughout the movement. If your gym has a captain's chair apparatus, lift yourself up, with your weight on your forearms. Holding the handles, lift your legs as with the hanging leg raise.

COMMENTS – Before raising and lowering your legs, be sure to flex your abs, lats and hip flexors while hanging to eliminate the possibility of your body using momentum to swing through the rep. Always attempt to raise your legs quickly and lower your legs slowly.

MUSCLES WORKED – Hanging leg raises thoroughly work your abs. Hip flexors, thighs and forearms will also be forced into play.

OBLIQUE CRUNCH

Lie on the floor with your knees bent and your feet firmly positioned on the floor. Keep your shoulders slightly elevated off the ground with your fingers barely touching behind your head. Slightly rotate your torso and shoulder towards your opposite knee and then return to the original position before doing the same movement with your other side. Avoid using momentum by performing the entire range of move-

ment in a slow fashion and by alternating between the two sides of your body.
COMMENTS – When performing this exercise, you should be attempting to point your left shoulder towards your right knee and vice versa.
MUSCLES WORKED – As the name would suggest, the oblique crunch primarily works the obliques, though the upper abs are also worked.

TWISTING CRUNCH

Lie on your back with your hands behind your head and rest your right ankle on your left knee. Raise your left shoulder and point your left elbow toward your right knee while twisting your torso in an inward and upward fashion. Lower your left shoulder to complete the rep. Follow these same instructions for the opposite side of your body, for the same number of reps.
COMMENTS – Because of the stance involved with this exercise, it's probably best to avoid alternating from one side to the next for each rep. Do all of your reps for one side and then immediately change your position and perform an equal amount of reps for the opposite side.
MUSCLES WORKED – The primary area worked with twisting crunches are the obliques, while the abs and hip flexors also receive significant stimulation.

KNEE-IN

Sit at the middle of a bench and lean back, resting your hands on the bench just behind your hips to support yourself. Slowly raise your legs and bend at the knees. At this point, when viewed from the side, your body should resemble a V shape and you should contract your abs and crunch your upper body slightly forward. Hold the position for a couple of seconds before returning your legs to the starting position.

COMMENTS – To increase the difficulty, hold a dumbbell that you feel comfortable enough to lift between your ankles.
MUSCLES WORKED – Knee-ins will primarily work your abs, though your arms will also receive some stimulation.

AB WHEEL ROLLOUT

Get into a kneeling position while holding the ab wheel against the floor with both hands. Extend your arms and slowly roll the ab wheel as far as possible in a forward motion. Once you've reached the furthest point possible, pause and reverse the action by pulling your arms and the ab wheel back to the starting point.
COMMENTS – Keep your core (lumbar spine and abs) locked throughout the exercise. If you've never performed this exercise, begin slowly (allowing your arms to stretch only to about a 45 degree angle) before advancing to greater angles.
MUSCLES WORKED – Working with the ab wheel will impact on your abs and lumbar spine muscles.

LEGS (THIGHS)
BARBELL SQUAT

Place the barbell on the squat rack, about shoulder height. Step under the bar and rest it across your traps and shoulders. Step away from the rack, placing your feet slightly less than shoulder-width apart. In a slow and controlled manner, bend your knees and descend towards the floor. Stop when your thighs are almost parallel to the floor. Pause for a second and return to the start position.
COMMENTS – Always wear a belt when performing squats and don't bounce at the top or bottom of the exercise. Control the weight throughout the movement. Keep your stance shoulder width or less because the wider the stance, the more glute assistance in lifting mas-

sive poundages. For beginners, try to use a squat rack with "catchers." These are pins that will stop the weight if you get into trouble. If none are available, have one or two spotters watching you (and they'll no doubt tell you if you're doing the exercise properly).

MUSCLES WORKED – While primarily a quad builder, squats will stimulate the whole leg region. Even with a narrow stance, the glutes come into play. Also, the calves and hamstrings are used in stabilizing the legs as you move up and down while the spinal erectors (lower back muscles) are needed to keep the body upright.

SMITH-MACHINE SQUAT

This exercise is performed in the same way as the barbell squat except it's done in a Smith machine.

COMMENTS – As with regular squats don't bounce at the bottom of the exercise. Try experimenting with different foot positions – both wide and narrow and forward and back. Smith-machine squats allow for change in the forward or backward stance, because you don't need to worry about the balance factor.

MUSCLES WORKED – Smith-machine squats primarily work the thighs and glutes, but the lower back, hamstrings, and calves also come into play.

LEG PRESS

Sit in a leg-press machine, placing your feet shoulder-width apart in the center of the footplate. Slowly lower the weight, bringing your knees to a 90-degree angle, pause and then press through your heels to full leg extension (knees unlocked). Perform the movement in a slow, controlled manner.

COMMENTS – Although leg presses don't give the same degree of thigh development as squats, they're a close second. If you have knee or back prob-

lems, the leg press will adequately work the thighs without aggravating these areas. By making a V with the feet (heels together, toes apart) you can do wonders with the inner thigh region. Perhaps the greatest advantage of leg presses is that you can pile on the plates.

MUSCLES WORKED – When performing the leg press most of the stress is on the thighs. There's very little glute involvement, and the spinal erectors are all but eliminated from the exercise. The calves and hamstrings play only a small role in stabilizing the legs during the exercise.

HACK SQUAT

In the hack-squat machine, position yourself by placing your feet about shoulder-width apart on the incline footplate. Slowly squat down until your hips and knees are parallel to the floor. Then press through your heels to lift the weight, returning to the starting position (knees unlocked).

COMMENTS - There are two variations of the hack machine. The version most bodybuilders prefer uses shoulder pads for supporting the weight. The other relies on two handles placed low on the machine.

To get the exercise's full benefit, make a slight V-shape with your feet (heels together, toes apart). Don't bounce at the bottom as this places tremendous strain on the knee ligaments.

MUSCLES WORKED – Hack squats will give your outer thighs that nice sweeping look.

LEG EXTENSION

Sit with your back pressed firmly on the back pad and place your feet under the padded rollers. Extend your legs to a locked position and contract your quads at the top. Slowly lower to the starting position and repeat.

COMMENTS – Some bodybuilders lie on

their backs when doing leg extensions. You can't use the same amount of weight, but you can work the quads through a greater range of motion. The downside is that there may be extra stress placed on the lower back.

Resist the tendency to drop the weight into the starting position, as 50% of the work is in the negative (lowering) phase of the exercise.

MUSCLES WORKED – Extensions are useful for building the quad muscles around the knee area. They are great for strengthening not only the lower quads, but also the associated tendons and ligaments.

SISSY SQUAT

With a shoulder-width stance grasp a support at your side and at hip level. Lean back, allow your heels to come off the floor and squat down until your thighs are at least parallel with the floor. If you can do 15 to 20 reps with relative ease, hold a plate with your free hand against the chest.

COMMENTS – You can do this exercise with a dumbbell or weight plate held to the chest. Don't get carried away with the amount of weight. This is a challenging exercise. Save the heavy poundage for your regular squats and leg presses.

MUSCLES WORKED – Sissy squats are similar to hack squats, in that they'll add a great sweep to your outer thighs. Although more isolated than regular squats, sissy squats involve the glutes to some degree.

DUMBELL or BARBELL LUNGE

Rest a barbell across the shoulders and step forward with your right leg, bending down until you have a 90-degree angle between the upper and lower legs. Try to keep a slight bend in the rear leg. Slowly return to the starting position and then step forward with your left leg. Repeat.

COMMENTS – Adjust your stance so that the knee of the forward leg doesn't go past the toes. Also try not to bounce in and out of the exercise as this places extra stress on the knees. For variety you can perform this exercise by holding two dumbbells in your hands.

MUSCLES WORKED – Like squats, lunges primarily work the thighs and glutes, but the hamstrings, lower back and calves, play a stabilizing role.

WALKING LUNGE

Grasp a dumbbell with each hand and let your arms hang completely straight by your sides with your palms facing inwards. Take one step forward with your right leg making a 90-degree angle at the knee, while lowering your left leg so that it extends behind you without allowing any portion of it (with the exception of your toes) to touch the floor. Hold in that position for a couple of seconds then take another step forward with the opposite leg.

COMMENTS – Avoid taking short steps. For stability and consistency, find a spacious place to perform this exercise in order to avoid having to turn around.

MUSCLES WORKED – Walking lunges primarily work your quads. Your hamstrings, inner thighs and glutes will also reap the rewards of this simple exercise.

LEGS (HAMSTRINGS)
LYING LEG CURL

Lie facedown on the leg curl machine, with your feet under the rollers. Keeping your hips down, use your hamstrings to curl your legs towards your buttocks. Pause at the top, and slowly lower back to the starting position.

COMMENTS – There are three variations of the leg curl machine. Two of them require you to lie facedown on either a straight or partly angled bench, the latter of which forces you to do the exercise more strictly. There is also a standing leg curl machine that allows you to work one leg at a time. Leg curls should be performed in a slow, rhythmic style.

MUSCLES WORKED – Leg curls primarily work the hamstrings, although there's some calf involvement. The glutes and thighs come into play only to stabilize the legs.

SEATED LEG CURL

Sit in a seated leg curl machine with your ankles on the ankle pad. Curl your lower legs under you and bring your feet as close to the bottom of the bench as possible. Hold for a second, squeeze your hamstrings, and then return your feet to the start.

COMMENTS – The advantage of the seated over the lying leg curl is strictness. It's very easy to cheat on the lying leg curl by lifting your hips or pulling with the arms. The seated leg curl forces you to move the weight with just your hamstrings.

MUSCLES WORKED – Seated leg curls primarily work the hamstrings, but the glutes and calves also play a small role.

STIFF-LEGGED DEADLIFT

Place an Olympic bar on the floor in front of a block of wood, or on the end of a flat bench. Stand on the block or bench and, with the legs slightly bent, grasp the bar with a shoulder-width grip and lift to standing position. Pause for a second, and then bend forward until the plates are just short of touching the floor.

COMMENTS – While the name says "stiff-legged," keeping the legs completely locked can put extra stress on the lower back. Keep a slight bend in the knees.

MUSCLES WORKED – Although the knees do not bend as in a traditional

deadlift, the hamstring muscles do cross the hip joint and are thus stimulated by extension at the hip. The lower spinal erectors and glutes also come into play with this exercise.

CHEST
FLAT-BENCH BARBELL PRESS

Lie on your back and take the barbell from the supports, using a grip that is six to eight inches wider than shoulder width. Lower the bar slowly to the nipple region, and then press it back to the locked out position.

COMMENTS – Don't bounce the bar off the chest. Although you can lift more weight this way, it's far less effective. To avoid injury, lower the weight in a slow, controlled manner, and then push it back to arms' length. Avoid arching your back, as it decreases the amount of pectoral stimulation and doesn't benefit your lower back.

MUSCLES WORKED – Flat-bench presses primarily work the lower chest region, but the whole pectoral-deltoid area is stimulated as well as your triceps. The back and forearm muscles are indirectly used for stabilizing the upper body during the exercise.

INCLINE DUMBBELL PRESS

Lie on an incline bench set to a fairly low angle. Hold the dumbbells just outside your shoulders and your elbows out to your sides. Press the weights up in an arc so they come together at the top of the movement and your arms are fully extended above your chest.

COMMENTS – Again, lower the dumbbells slowly, and go for a full, but controlled stretch at the bottom.

MUSCLES WORKED – Incline dumbbell presses are an excellent exercise for developing the upper chest. Because of the increased angle, they also hit the front deltoids. As with most chest exercises, there's some secondary triceps involvement. If your shoulders are taking too much of the weight, drop the bench angle a few degrees.

CHEST DIP
Most gyms have a set of parallel bars for doing dips. Start the exercise with your arms in a locked-out position. Lean forward, bend your knees and with your elbows out to your sides bend them to lower your body down between the bars until your arms are parallel to the floor. Pause, and then push yourself back up.
COMMENTS – To keep the stress on the chest, lean forward and flare your elbows out to the side. If you keep vertical and have your elbows in tight, the exercise is more of a triceps builder. As with other chest exercises, don't bounce at the bottom.
MUSCLES WORKED – Dips primarily work the lower, outer chest. They produce that clean line under the pecs. They also stimulate the front delts and triceps.

INCLINE DUMBBELL FLYE
Begin with an incline bench set at a 30- to 45-degree angle. Lie on the bench with your feet flat and back pressed against the pad. Hold the dumbbells with your arms straight and palms facing each other. Slowly lower your arms out to your sides, pause at the bottom, and then squeeze the dumbbells up and together, over the center of the chest.
COMMENTS – As with incline dumbbell presses, the incline bench dictates lifting the dumbbells higher. You may need a partner to hoist the dumbbells into position. Jerking heavy dumbbells from the floor puts a great deal of stress on the biceps and lower back.
MUSCLES WORKED –Incline flyes put most of the stress on the upper pectorals. They also strongly affect your chest-shoulder tie-ins.

CABLE CROSSOVER
Stand between the two cable uprights and grasp an overhead pulley handle in each hand. Adopt a runner's stance (one leg forward and the other back and slightly bent) and, with your arms slightly bent, bring the handles forward and down to about your midsection. Pause a moment, squeezing your pecs, and return to the start.
COMMENTS – Be sure to return to the start in a slow and controlled manner. If you let your arms fly back you run the risk of tearing the pec-delt tie-in. To ease the stress on the shoulder joint, keep a slight bend in the elbows. This exercise can also be done from the floor, using a lower pulley instead of the overhead.
MUSCLES WORKED – Cable crossovers work the center of the chest and front delts.

PEC-DECK
Sit in a pec-deck machine and grasp the handles or place the forearms behind the pads. Flex your pecs and push the arms forward until the handles or pads are just about touching. Squeeze your pecs and slowly return to the starting position.
COMMENTS – Don't allow your arms to fly back too fast or you can tear the chest or shoulders. Use as little arm power as possible; instead think of the arms as extensions of your chest muscles.
MUSCLES WORKED – Pec-deck flyes hit the inner chest and pec-deck tie-ins.

DECLINE DUMBBELL PRESS
With dumbbells in each hand and your feet firmly locked in place just under the pads at the end of the bench, lie back. Turn your elbows so they are parallel to your shoulders and with explosive force press the dumbbells as high as possible. To complete the rep, slowly lower the dumbbells to the starting position and pause briefly in that posi-

Photo by Jason Breeze
Model Lou Joseph

tion before beginning the next rep.

COMMENTS – When performing each rep, imagine lifting the dumbbells in a triangular direction. Your head, shoulders and butt should remain pressed against the bench throughout the exercise.

MUSCLES WORKED – Decline dumbbell presses will greatly impact on your lower pec muscles, and to a lesser extent your upper pecs, triceps and shoulders.

PUSH-UP

With your body in a perfectly straight line, put both hands on the ground directly under your shoulders and prop up the lower end of your body with your toes and feet together. Lower your body by bending at the elbows and hold that position for a couple of seconds before pressing back up to the original starting position and completing the rep.

COMMENTS – Always perform each rep slowly and resist the temptation to use the assistance of momentum or your shoulders.

MUSCLES WORKED – The primary area being worked with a push-up is the pectorals. The deltoids, rear triceps and wrists will also come into play.

PUSH-UP ON HANDLES

Securely place a set of push-up handles on the ground. Keeping your feet together and your arms stretched out greater than shoulder-width apart, place your hands on a set of push-up handles. Slowly lower your body by bending your elbows as with a regular push-up. Hold the position for a couple of seconds before completing the rep by powering your body up and returning to the starting position.

COMMENTS – If you experience wrist pain performing standard push-ups, push-up handles can help as they can significantly alter wrist angles to accommodate your injuries.

MUSCLES WORKED – The pectoral muscles are the primary muscles worked by push-ups on handles. The deltoids and triceps are also significantly worked.

BACK
CHIN-UP

Grasp the bar with a shoulder-width underhand grip and hang with arms extended. Pull yourself up by squeezing your shoulder blades together and contracting your lats. Hold for a second and then lower back down to the starting position in a controlled manner.

COMMENTS – Chins help to create a great V-shape. When doing the movement, try to pull with the large back muscles (latissimus dorsi), not the biceps and forearms. When you're able to do 12 to 15 easy reps, attach a weight around your waist or hold a dumbbell between your legs. This increases the resistance and keeps the muscles growing.

MUSCLES WORKED – Chins primarily work the large lat muscles. They also stress the smaller back muscles such as the teres major and minor. The rear delts and biceps are also brought into play.

LAT PULLDOWN TO FRONT

Using a lat-pulldown machine, take an overhand wide grip (about twice your shoulder width) on a lat bar attached to a pulley. Pull the bar down to the front and touch your chest. Pause at the bottom and return to the outstretched arms position.

COMMENTS – Keep your grip fairly wide, as narrow grip pulldowns place more stress on the biceps. This exercise can also be performed with a reverse grip.

MUSCLES WORKED – Lat pulldowns work the entire back region, from the large latissimus muscles to the smaller teres, rhomboids and rear deltoids. They also stress the biceps and forearms.

BENT-OVER BARBELL ROW

Bend forward at the waist so your upper body is just short of parallel to the floor. Grasp a standard barbell and, using a wide overhand grip, pull it up toward the abdomen. Lower slowly and then repeat. Concentrate on using the upper back muscles (lats).

COMMENTS – Keep in mind that your upper body and legs should remain stationary throughout the exercise. Also make sure you bend your knees slightly to help reduce the stress on your lower back.

MUSCLES WORKED –Besides the back muscles, bent-over rows stress the biceps and forearms. Also because of the bent-over position, the exercise stretches the hamstrings and spinal erectors.

T-BAR ROW

T-bar rows are an effective substitute for the barbell version. Grasp the crossbar with an overhand grip, bend at the hips and pull the plates up to the chest/abdominal region. Squeeze at the top and then lower to a full stretch at the bottom.

COMMENTS – Keep your upper body stationary and lift the plates with only your back muscles and arms. If you have lower back problems, you might want to avoid T-bar rows. If you must do them, start off by using light weights and gradually build up the poundage.

MUSCLES WORKED – T-bar rows work the same muscles as the regular barbell row. The lats, teres, rhomboids, rear delts, biceps, forearms and lower back, all come into play.

SEATED ROW

Sit on a cable row bench with your feet firmly planted on the footplate. Grasp the double-D pulley attachment. With your legs slightly bent, pull the handle toward your midsection. Pause for a second and squeeze the shoulder blades together. Now bend forward and stretch the arms out fully.

COMMENTS – You can perform this exercise with a number of different pulley attachments. Some bodybuilders like to use a straight pulldown bar or two separate handgrips.

MUSCLES WORKED – Seated pulley rows are another exercise that works the whole back region. They are more of a thickness movement than a width builder. They also stimulate the biceps and forearms.

ONE-ARM ROW

Grasp a dumbbell in one hand. Rest your other hand and same-side leg on the bench for support. The other foot is on the ground for balance. Pull the dumbbell up your side until your elbow is fully bent.

COMMENTS – Even though your biceps will be involved in the exercise, try to concentrate on using just your back muscles.

MUSCLES WORKED – The primary muscles worked are the lats. The secondary muscles are the rhomboids, teres major, traps and biceps.

STRAIGHT-ARM LAT PUSHDOWN or PULLDOWN

Stand two to three feet in front of the lat pulldown machine. Grasp the attached bar with a shoulder-width overhand grip. Your arms should be in front, arms straight. Push the bar down to your thighs and then slowly return the bar to the start.

COMMENTS – If you're tall you may find the plates touch before you get a good stretch at the top of the exercise. In that case simply stand farther back or adopt a wide stance. The wider your stance the lower you'll go to the floor.

MUSCLES WORKED – This exercise hits the upper and outer lats, just under the armpits. Straight-arm pushdowns make

Photo by Robert Reiff
Model Joel Stubbs

an excellent first exercise in a pre-exhaust superset.

BARBELL DEADLIFT

With your feet directly below the bar, squat down and, using an overhand grip, place your hands slightly wider than shoulder-width apart. With the bar barely brushing up against your shins and your chest in an upright position, slowly move to a standing position while making sure to keep your arms perfectly straight as you lift the barbell. Keep your chin up and look forward throughout the rep. Reverse the action to complete the rep.

COMMENTS – Be sure to squeeze the muscles in your legs, glutes and back while performing each rep.

MUSCLES WORKED – The area primarily targeted when performing the barbell deadlift is the lower back. Glutes, inner thighs, quads and calves will also receive significant stimulation.

BENT-OVER CABLE ROW

Stand directly in front of a low pulley cable machine and grasp the cable handles. With your feet about shoulder-width apart, bend your knees, brace your abs and slightly arch your lower back. Pull the cable back until your arms almost touch your midsection and then slowly return the cable to its starting position by straightening your arm to complete the rep.

COMMENTS – To get the most out of this exercise, tense the middle of your back before returning the cable to the starting position.

MUSCLES WORKED – Bent-over cable rows primarily work the lats, but also impact on the scapular retractors, posterior deltoids, hip extensors and spinal extensors.

CLOSE-GRIP LAT PULLDOWN

Sit with your knees resting comfort-ably beneath the pull-down machine's roller supports and your feet spread roughly shoulder-width apart. Raise your arms and pull the double-D attachment with both of your hands to just under your neck. Pause briefly in this position before slowly returning the attachment to its original overhead position.

COMMENTS – Be sure to lift your sternum and lean back prior to beginning the workout, but don't lean back too far – doing so could inadvertently create momentum that may assist you during the rep.

MUSCLES WORKED – A close-grip lat pulldown not only impacts on the lats, but to a lesser extent it also affects the forearms, biceps, pecs and rhomboids.

ONE-ARM CABLE ROW (LAWNMOWER PULL)

With your knees slightly bent stand in front of a low pulley cable machine and grasp the handle with your palm facing down. Pretend that you're about to start up your lawnmower and, with your body as straight as possible, slowly pull the handle toward your chest. Once you reach your chest, stop and slowly return the handle to the original position to conclude the rep.

COMMENTS – The cable should be at about shoulder level. To avoid injury as well as get the most out of the exercise, don't let the pressure from the cable allow you to quickly snap back into the starting position.

MUSCLES WORKED – The one-arm cable row primarily works the lats, but also impacts on the biceps.

PULL-UP (from hanging)

Grasp the pull-up bar with an overhand grip and your hands about shoulder-width apart. With your arms completely extended and hanging from the pull-up bar, pull your body up. To perform a proper pull-up, imagine that you are forcing your shoulder blades together. At the same time you should be using your lats to help you lift your body up to the point where your chin just surpasses the pull-up bar. Slowly lower your body back to the original position.

COMMENTS – To shock and confuse your muscles into greater growth, be sure to vary your grip technique (using anything from a close to wide grip).

MUSCLES WORKED – Pull-ups provide an excellent upper body workout, impacting on the lats, pecs, abs, shoulders, biceps and forearms.

WEIGHTED PULL-UP

Securely fasten a weight belt around your waist. The belt should have a weight attached to it that you'll feel comfortable enough performing your desired reps with. Grasp the pull-up bar using an overhand grip. Keep your hands about shoulder-width apart. Pull your body up to the point where your neck is roughly parallel to the pull-up bar and then slowly lower your body to the starting position.

COMMENTS – The added weight involved will force greater muscle growth than a standard pull-up. If you don't have a weight belt, you could also place a dumbbell between your ankles.

MUSCLES WORKED – The primary muscles being worked with weighted pull-ups are the lats. Weighted pull-ups will also work the biceps, abs, forearms, neck, shoulders, lower traps and pecs.

BACK EXTENSION

Get into a back extension machine by resting your quadriceps against the pads and locking your feet into the base. With your hands pressed against the sides of your head or cradling a weight plate against your chest, bend forward until your lower back muscles feel a slight tightness. Hold that position for a couple of seconds and then slowly return to the starting position.

COMMENTS – To avoid the possibility of hyperextending your back it's important that when concluding a rep, you never arch your back past the starting position.

MUSCLES WORKED – Back extensions primarily work your lower back, but glutes and thigh muscles are also affected.

SHOULDERS
SHOULDER PRESS

With a slightly wider than shoulder-width overhand grip, unrack the barbell and lower the bar behind your head, stopping just short of your traps. Push the bar straight up overhead until your arms are straight but not locked. Slowly lower to the starting position.

COMMENTS – To complete this exercise use either the squat rack or the shoulder press rack. Most gyms have a special seat with a vertical back support.

MUSCLES WORKED – Behind-the-head presses work the entire shoulder region, particularly the front and side delts. They also stress, to a lesser degree, the rear delts, traps and triceps.

DUMBBELL OVERHEAD PRESS

Hold a pair of dumbbells at shoulder height. You can do this exercise seated or standing. With your palms facing forward, push the weights straight up, stopping just short of lockout. Lower the dumbbells in a slow and controlled motion.

COMMENTS – You can press both dumbbells at the same time or in an alternating fashion. Try not to excessively arch the lower back.

MUSCLES WORKED – This exercise

stresses the whole deltoid region. Particular emphasis is placed on the front and side deltoids with secondary trap and rear deltoid involvement.

BARBELL SHRUG

Grasp a barbell and hold at your thighs using a shoulder-width grip. Using your trapezius muscles, raise your shoulders by shrugging and try to touch your ears. Squeeze at the top of the movement, and then lower the bar down.

COMMENTS – For variety, instead of shrugging your shoulders in a straight line, you can rotate them in a circular direction. Try to keep the arms, legs and back straight throughout the movement, and watch the lower back.

MUSCLES WORKED – Barbell shrugs are by far the best trapezius builder. Besides the traps, your forearms, hamstrings, lower back and rear delts will be indirectly stimulated.

UPRIGHT ROW

Start the exercise by holding a barbell across the front of your thighs. Using a narrow grip, lift the bar up the front of the body, keeping the elbows flared to the sides. Squeeze the traps together at the top, and then lower into the starting position.

COMMENTS – If you have weak or injured wrists, you might want to avoid this exercise. Upright rows place tremendous stress on the forearms and wrists. If you experience minor pain when doing the exercise, try wrapping the wrists with support bandages.

MUSCLES WORKED – With a narrow grip, upright rows primarily work the traps, with some secondary deltoid stimulation. A wide grip (six inches or more) will shift the strain to the side delts, with the traps playing a secondary role. The forearms are worked regardless of grip.

Photo by Paul Buceta
Model Leo Ingram

DUMBBELL LATERAL RAISE

You can perform this exercise seated or standing. Grasp a pair of dumbbells and, with elbows slightly bent, lift them to the side of the body. As you lift the dumbbells, gradually rotate the wrists so your pinky fingers point up. Many bodybuilding authorities, including Robert Kennedy, liken this wrist action to pouring a jug of water.

COMMENTS – You can do the exercise with your arms completely locked, but most find it more effective to bend the arms slightly and use more weight. Instead of using dumbbells, a cable can also be substituted, by attaching a D-handle to a low pulley. Either version may be performed with one or two arms at a time.

MUSCLES WORKED – You can use lateral raises to work any head of the deltoid muscle. Most bodybuilders use them for the side delts, as the front delts receive ample stimulation from various pressing movements.

BENT-OVER DUMBBELL LATERAL RAISE

You can do this exercise free standing, seated or even lying prone. Stand with your knees slightly bent. Holding a pair of dumbbells in front of you, palms facing each other, bend forward and slowly lift the dumbbells up and out to your sides. Pause at the top and then slowly bring them back to the start.

COMMENTS – Concentrate on lifting the dumbbells with your rear delts and not your traps and lats. For variation try using a set of cables. Grasp the cable handles with your opposite hands, so the cables form an X in front of you at the start.

MUSCLES WORKED – When performed properly, bent-over laterals primarily work the rear deltoids, but it also works the triceps, traps and lats.

FRONT DUMBBELL RAISE

Grasp two dumbbells and, with your palms facing the floor and arms locked straight, slowly lift them to shoulder height (arms parallel to the floor). Slowly return the dumbbells to the hips.

COMMENTS – There are a number of different variations of this exercise. Some people find it easier to keep the palms facing inwards or upwards. You can also alternate lifting the dumbbells as opposed to both at the same time.

MUSCLES WORKED – Front raises primarily work the front deltoids, but the biceps, side and rear deltoids receive secondary stimulation.

REVERSE PEC-DECK

Sit down in the pec-deck machine facing the backrest. Either grasp the handles or place your forearms in front of the pads. Bring your arms back to a comfortable stretch, which for most people means having the elbows slightly behind the body, or your arms straight out to the sides. Return to the starting position.

COMMENTS – Although you're using a pec-deck machine, the objective isn't to work your chest, but rather your rear delts. To ensure proper execution of the movement, your hands and shoulders should be aligned.

MUSCLES WORKED – Reverse pec flyes primarily hit the rear delts, as well as the teres, rhomboids and traps.

INTERNAL ROTATION

Lie on your side on a standard flat bench holding a dumbbell with the arm closest to the bench. Bend your arm at the elbow so it makes a 90-degree angle. Lower your forearm toward the floor until your forearm is just hanging off the bench and then slowly rotate your arm until your forearm completely crosses over your midsection. To complete the rep, lower your arm back to the starting position

COMMENTS – Rehab professionals typically suggest that patients suffering from rotator cuff injuries perform this exercise as part of their treatments.

MUSCLES WORKED – Internal rotations primarily work the rotator cuff, though the pectoral muscles, lats and anterior deltoid are also involved.

ARNOLD PRESS

Sit on a flat bench holding two dumbbells up with your palms facing your neck and your elbows directly beneath your wrists. Raise and rotate your arms by bringing your elbows wide and out to the sides of your body as you press the dumbbells high above your head. At this point, your palms should be facing the opposite direction and the dumbbells should almost meet yet not actually touch. Hold that position for a couple of seconds before you slowly lower the dumbbells to the starting position using the exact path as you did on the ascent.

COMMENTS – To avoid injury, use less weight when performing Arnold presses than you do when performing dumbbell presses, as Arnold presses require a greater range of motion.

MUSCLES WORKED – Arnold presses primarily work the anterior deltoid muscles, though the lateral deltoid, triceps, rotator cuff as well as the middle and lower trapezius muscles will also come into play.

BENT-OVER CABLE LATERAL RAISE

Bend your knees and stand with your feet slightly more than shoulder-width apart and the low cable pulley at your side. Using the arm furthest away from the machine, grasp the cable and with your arm remaining in a bent position, raise the cable. Bring the cable up to the point where your upper arm becomes parallel with your torso. Slowly return your arm back to the starting position.

COMMENTS – To maintain proper balance, rest your non-working hand on your upper thigh.

MUSCLES WORKED – Bent-over cable lateral raises primarily work the rear deltoids. Triceps muscles will also experience some stimulation.

EXTERNAL ROTATION

Lie on your side on a standard flat bench while holding a dumbbell in the hand of your free side (furthest from the bench). Position the arm holding the dumbbell at a 90-degree angle with your upper arm pressed against your side and your lower arm extending directly in front of your body. Before beginning the rep, lower your arm so the forearm rests against your midsection. Keeping your upper arm against your side and maintaining the 90-degree angle, externally rotate your lower arm until that portion of your arm reaches a vertical position. Hold that position for a couple of seconds and then slowly lower your arm to the starting position to begin the next rep.

COMMENTS – To avoid a rotator cuff injury, be sure to select poundage that will allow you to perform this exercise without straining.

MUSCLES WORKED – External rotations primarily help build muscular shoulders, though forearm and back muscles are also impacted.

WIDE-GRIP UPRIGHT ROW

Stand with your feet at least shoulder-width apart and hold the barbell with a wide overhand grip. The barbell should be resting directly in front of your thighs and your knees should be very slightly bent. Keeping the barbell close to your body throughout the rep, pull it up to your chin and hold that position briefly before returning the weight to the starting position.

COMMENTS – The wide-grip upright row forces your middle and front delts to exert far more effort than an ordinary narrow-grip upright row.

MUSCLES WORKED – Wide-grip upright rows will work your front and middle deltoids. Your rotator cuff, biceps, forearms, back and traps will also receive stimulation.

TRICEPS
TRICEPS PRESSDOWN

Stand facing a high-pulley cable with a pressdown bar attachment. Grasp the bar with an overhand grip. With your elbows tight to your sides, press the bar down to a locked-out position. Pause and contract the triceps at the bottom, and then return the bar to about chest height.

COMMENTS – Resist the urge to flare your elbows out to the sides. If you have to use momentum to push the bar down, you're probably pressing too much weight. You can use different attachments when performing this exercise such as a V-bar, rope etc.

MUSCLES WORKED – Triceps pressdowns work the entire triceps region, especially the outer head.

DUMBBELL OVERHEAD EXTENSION

Grasp a single dumbbell and extend it straight overhead. Keeping your upper arm stationary, lower the dumbbell behind your head to get a good stretch and then lift to full-arm extension. Try to perform the movement in a slow rhythmic manner.

COMMENTS – Never bounce the dumbbell at the bottom of the exercise. This exercise can also be performed by grasping the dumbbell with two hands.

MUSCLES WORKED – Although it works the whole triceps region, this exercise is great for the lower triceps.

LYING TRICEPS EXTENSION (SKULLCRUSHER)

Place an EZ-curl bar on the end of a bench. Lie face up on a flat bench with your feet flat on the floor. Hold a barbell at full-arm extension over your chest. Keeping your elbows by your sides, lower the bar to your forehead, and then return to the start.

COMMENTS – If you're wary about lowering the bar to your head, lower it to lightly touch the bench. Don't bounce the bar, but merely pause and then extend the arms.

MUSCLES WORKED – This stresses the whole triceps, particularly the long rear head of the muscle. Lowering the bar behind your head brings the lower lats and upper chest into play. The exercise also works the intercostals, located just beneath the ribcage.

PARALLEL-BAR DIP

Use a set of parallel bars as you would with the chest dip. Shift the work from the chest to the triceps by keeping the elbows tight against the body Also, keep your body as upright as possible. In fact some bodybuilders lean back slightly to get that extra degree of triceps stimulation.

COMMENTS – To increase the resistance, do a weighted dip by holding a dumbbell between your legs or by attaching a plate to a special dipping chain. Be careful at the bottom of the movement. Although dips are an excellent triceps exercise, they also place much stress on the front delts, particularly the pec-delt tie-in.

MUSCLES WORKED – Performed in an upright manner, dips place most of the strain on the long rear head of the triceps.

BENCH DIP

Place two benches about four feet apart. Rest the heels of your feet on one and

the heels of your hands on another. Slowly lower your body between the benches by bending at the elbows. Slowly return to the starting position so your arms are locked out.

COMMENTS – As with upright bar dips, the key to this exercise is to keep the torso leaning back and elbows close to the sides. As soon as the torso tilts forward and the elbows flare out, the larger chest muscles take over. To make this exercise more difficult have a partner add weight plates on your lap.

MUSCLES WORKED – This exercise works the triceps primarily and the delts and lats second. The traps, biceps, pecs and mid-back are also involved.

ONE-ARM REVERSE CABLE PRESSDOWN

With your body in the standing, upright position, grasp the handle with an underhand grip and hold it at chest level with your elbow close to your side. Keeping your upper arm stationary, straighten your arm until it's fully extended. Pause and then return to the starting position.

COMMENTS – You can also perform this exercise with a palms-down grip.

MUSCLES WORKED – A palms-up grip will place most of the strain on the rear triceps. It also targets the shoulders, back and chest muscles.

CLOSE-GRIP BENCH PRESS

Lie down on a flat bench with an Olympic bar or EZ-curl bar placed on the supports above you. Grasp the bar with a narrow (shoulder width or less) grip and lower it down to mid-chest, keeping your elbows as close to your sides as possible. Press the bar back up to the start.

COMMENTS – You'll need to experiment with different grip widths to find the one that maximizes triceps involvement and minimizes wrist stress. Don't bounce the

bar off your chest or arch your lower back.

MUSCLES WORKED – Close-grip presses primarily work the triceps but the front delts and pecs also come into play.

ONE-ARM REVERSE CABLE EXTENSION

Attach a rope to the pulldown machine and set the pulley wheel just slightly above your head. Grasp the rope with both hands and turn around so your back is to the machine. Lean forward and adopt a runner's stance (one leg forward and slightly bent and the other back and relatively straight). With the upper arms kept parallel to the floor and elbows in line with your ears, slowly extend your arms to a locked-out position. Slowly return to the starting position by bending your elbows. Your hands should be just behind your head at the end.

COMMENTS – Try not to "throw" the body into the movement as this reduces the amount of triceps stimulation. Keep your legs bent to reduce the stress on your lower back. You can also perform this exercise with a short straight bar or an EZ-curl bar.

MUSCLES WORKED – Like most extension exercises, rope extensions target the whole triceps, particularly the long rear head.

REVERSE CABLE EXTENSION

Standing directly in front of a cable extension machine, grasp the bar with your hands roughly shoulder-width apart and both palms facing you. Start with the bar at shoulder level and lower it until your arms are completely straight. To complete the rep, slowly return the bar to the starting position.

COMMENTS – Avoid swinging your arms or using momentum while performing this exercise by keeping your elbows snug against your sides.

MUSCLES WORKED – The triceps are the main area worked by reverse cable extensions though the forearms will also come into play.

BICEPS
BARBELL CURL

Grasp the bar with a shoulder-width grip and with your elbows close to your sides. Curl the bar up toward your shoulders. Pause at the top, squeeze your biceps and lower the weight back to the starting position.

COMMENTS – The negative part of the movement is just as important as the positive. Keep your back straight and don't swing the weight. You can use the standard Olympic bar, a smaller straight bar or an EZ-curl bar. The latter bar's bent shape allows you to rotate your forearms slightly, thus reducing the tension on the wrists and forearms.

MUSCLES WORKED – The barbell biceps curl works the entire biceps muscle. Also, because you have to forcibly grip the bar, the exercise will give you a great set of forearms. The front delts and lower back come into play for stabilizing purposes.

STANDING DUMBBELL CURL

Stand with your feet shoulder-width apart and knees slightly bent. Grasp a pair of dumbbells with an underhand grip and slowly curl them toward your shoulders. Pause at the top, squeeze your biceps and then return the weights to the start position. You can also perform alternating dumbbell curls, where you curl the dumbbells one at a time. As you curl, rotate your palms from the facing-in position to a facing-up position. This is called supination.

COMMENTS – Concentrate on each and every rep. Although Arnold favored the alternating version, choose the version that feels most productive.

MUSCLES WORKED – Dumbbell curls are great for working the belly of the biceps. They also reduce the stress on the wrists and forearms.

PREACHER CURL

Also called Scott curls, this exercise is great for working the lower biceps region. Start by sitting on the stool or bench connected to the preacher board. Adjust yourself so the padded board fits snugly under your upper arms. Take the barbell (straight or EZ-bar) from the supports with an underhand grip and curl it toward your shoulders. Lower to the start position and repeat.

COMMENTS – Some preacher benches are positioned fairly high and require you to stand up when doing the movement. If your gym has both, give both a try and pick the one that suits you best.

MUSCLES WORKED – Although they work the whole biceps muscle, preacher curls are mainly a peaking exercise. There's also some forearm stimulation.

INCLINE DUMBBELL CURL

Set an incline bench to at least 45 degrees. Lie back on the bench and grasp two dumbbells with an underhand grip. Curl the dumbbells up toward your shoulders, and then return to the start.

COMMENTS – Once again you have the option of curling both dumbbells simultaneously or alternately. The advantage of the incline bench is that it limits the amount of cheating you can do.

MUSCLES WORKED – Incline curls work the whole biceps region. Many bodybuilders find that they are great for bringing out the biceps peak. The exercise does provide some forearm stimulation, but not to the extent as the various barbell curls.

CONCENTRATION CURL

Sit down on the end of a bench with your

Photo by Gregory James
Model Lee Banks

feet shoulder-width apart. Grasp a dumb-bell, and with your elbow resting on your inner thigh, lower the dumbbell down, and then curl it back up. Perform one set, and then switch arms.

COMMENTS – Most bodybuilders perform concentration curls in the seated position. Arnold Schwarzenegger is known for performing them in the standing, bent-over position. Instead of bracing the elbow against the thigh, it's held down and away from the body. Keep the shoulder on the working side, lower than the free side. Resist the urge to swing and use only biceps power.

MUSCLES WORKED – This exercise primarily works the lower biceps. Most bodybuilders consider concentration curls more a shaping and peaking exercise than a mass builder.

EZ-BAR CURL

Standing straight, grasp the EZ-bar with an underhand grip and your hands shoulder-width apart. Curl the bar until your arms reach a vertical position and the bar is parallel to your shoulders. Hold the position for a couple of seconds and then slowly lower the EZ-bar to complete the rep.

COMMENTS – Your elbows should remain close to your sides throughout the exercise.

MUSCLES WORKED – The main muscles being worked while performing EZ-bar curls are the biceps, though forearms will also be impacted.

HAMMER CURL

Standing straight, grasp a dumbbell with each hand and, with your palms facing each other, hold the dumbbells by your sides. Raise your forearms and stop when they are parallel to the ground. At this point squeeze your forearms and biceps before returning the dumbbells to the starting position to complete the rep.

COMMENTS – Keep your abs tight and your elbows by your sides throughout the exercise. Avoid using momentum.

MUSCLES WORKED – Hammer curls primarily work the biceps, forearms, brachialis and brachioradialis.

CALVES
STANDING CALF RAISE

Stand under the shoulder pads of a calf raise machine. Place the balls of your feet at the edge of the footrest. With your legs locked, rise up and down on your toes, making sure to contract the calf muscles.

COMMENTS –Keep your back and legs straight. The only movement should be at the ankle joint. Although calf injuries are extremely rare you still shouldn't bounce at the bottom of the movement, as you might strain your Achilles tendon.

MUSCLES WORKED – Standing calf raises work the entire calf muscle, with the primary focus on the upper (gastrocnemius) calf region.

TOE PRESS

Sit in a leg press machine. Instead of pressing the weight with your feet and quads, press the weight up using your toes and contracting your calf muscles, keeping your knees straight. Pause at the top and then lower your heels back to the start.

COMMENTS – The advantage of this exercise is that you don't have the entire weight pushing down on your spine. This exercise is an adequate substitute if you don't have access to a standing calf machine.

MUSCLES WORKED – Most of the stress is placed on the gastrocnemius, but the soleus is also worked. If you want to get that extra burn in the lower calf, use less weight and bend your legs slightly. This will shift the stress to the soleus.

Photo by Paul Buceta
Model Steve Kuclo

SEATED CALF RAISE

Sit in a seated calf machine, placing your feet on the edge of the footrest and your knees under the pads. Lift your heels to raise the weight as high as you can on the balls of your feet, and then lower, letting your heels drop to get a good stretch.

COMMENTS – Because it works the lower calf, you'll need to use less weight. Go for at least 20 reps and try to feel every one of them. Don't bounce the weight on your legs. Even though the supports are padded, improper style can injure your knees.

MUSCLES WORKED – Since your legs are bent, most of the stress is placed on the lower calf (soleus), but there's some secondary, upper-calf involvement.

CALF RAISE ON HACK SQUAT MACHINE

Position your shoulders directly under the resistance pads. Your feet should be firmly planted on the footplate, close together, but not touching. Your legs and back should remain as straight as possible throughout the exercise. Slowly lift your heels off the floor until you are standing way up on your toes. To complete the rep, lower your heels until they have just barely touched the footplate.

COMMENTS – If you bend your knees while performing this exercise, you can also work on your quadriceps muscles.

MUSCLES WORKED – If you are executing this move properly, the only muscles being worked are the calves.

WRISTS
WRIST CURL

Grasp a dumbbell with one hand and sit near the middle of a bench. Allow your forearm to lay flat across the bench with your hand, wrist and the dumbbell hanging over the end of the bench. Curl the dumbbell upwards. On the decline portion of the rep, be sure to allow the dumbbell to roll toward your fingertips.

COMMENTS – This exercise is among the most effective in enhancing your grip strength. Use a lighter weight to prevent forearm and wrist injuries.

MUSCLES WORKED – The wrist curl is used to work the wrist flexors.

WRIST ROLLER

Hold the bar at chest level, arms out front and slightly bent at the elbow. Begin rolling the bar backwards. Once the weight plate reaches the bar, then begin rolling the bar forward until the plate touches the ground and you've completed one rep.

COMMENTS – If you don't own a wrist roller, it's easy enough to make your own. Simply find a rope, attach a weight plate to one end of the rope and attach a bar or stick to the other end.

MUSCLES WORKED – The main areas worked with the wrist roller are the forearms and wrists, though the shoulders are also affected.

REVERSE WRIST CURL

Sit at the end of a bench and grasp a dumbbell with your palm facing down. Rest your forearm across your leg so your wrist hangs just off of your knee. Lower and raise the dumbbell as much as possible without allowing your forearm to leave your leg. Return to the starting position to perform the next rep.

COMMENTS – By performing this exercise sitting on a bench, you're better able to stabilize your arms and in turn get the most beneficial wrist exercise possible.

MUSCLES WORKED – The wrist extensors are the only muscles receiving significant stimulation when performing reverse wrist curls.

INDEX

Photo by Jason Breeze
Model Chris White

Photo by Gregory James
Models Peter Putnam and Andy Haman

Photo by Paul Buceta
Model Lee Priest

Photo by Paul Buceta
Model Robert Burneika

N

O

P

Photo by Gregory James
Model Mark Dugdale